The Conspiracy
CONSPIRACY

How to fool all of the people all of the time!

DAVID BRYANT

THE CONSPIRACY CONSPIRACY
Copyright © 2018 David Bryant. All rights reserved.
First paperback edition printed 2018 in the United Kingdom.
A catalogue record for this book is available from the British Library.

ISBN 978-1-9997417-1-6

No part of this book shall be reproduced or transmitted in any form or by any means,
electronic or mechanical, including photocopying, recording, or by any information retrieval system
without written permission of the publisher.

Published by
Heathland Books

For more copies of this book, please email: info@spacerocksuk.com
Telephone: 01603 715933
Designed and typeset by Bob Tibbitts
Printed in Great Britain

Although every precaution has been taken in the preparation of this book,
the publisher and author assume no responsibility for errors or omissions.
Neither is any liability assumed for damages resulting from the use of this
information contained within.

Dedication

To Linda:
My Best Friend and Inspiration

Contents

Foreword vii

Introduction xi

Chapter 1: A spoonful of sugar? 1

Chapter 2: Education or indoctrination? 23

Chapter 3: Applied Science! 39

Chapter 4: The Conservation Game 67

Chapter 5: No more heroes 87

Chapter 6: The truth, the whole truth and anything but the truth 97

Chapter 7: Don't shoot the messenger! 117

Chapter 8: Conspiracy theories that refuse to go away 125

Chapter 9: In conclusion 153

Appendix 1	157
Appendix 2	161
Appendix 3	165
Acknowledgments and Thanks	169
Bibliography	171
Glossary	173

Foreword

by Ray Kohn

THERE are some authors who write in such a conversational style that you can believe that they are chatting to you. David Bryant has that engaging way of communicating, making this book very easy to read. There are passages when he describes his personal experiences bird watching or teaching that illustrate his arguments persuasively. **The Conspiracy Conspiracy** seeks to show that it is possible to fool most of the people most of the time. David, of course, seeks to escape that charge by putting forward arguments that he feels will stick in the craw of those with power.

There are chapters where he writes with authority. The way that the education sector in the UK has been dysfunctional is a theme that runs back to Ivan Illich's 'Deschooling Society' and my own Fabian Tract 'Enforced Leisure: enforced education' – both of which were written about 40 years ago. David shows that little has changed in the intervening decades and that the cynical way that those in power have attempted to manipulate schooling with little or no regard for teachers and pupils tars politicians of all parties. Demonstrating his arguments from his own experience gives this chapter significant credence.

The Conservation Game is a chapter where, again, the author's personal experience should bring weight to his observations. Head of Environmental, Rural and Agricultural Sciences at a large Norfolk High School and an avid twitcher, David Bryant launches a swingeing attack on all those who would dismiss any causation to global warming that was not simply down to human generation of carbon dioxide. Again, looking at those people and businesses that benefit from the creation of the 'green' industry, he questions why alternative explanations are dismissed so readily.

Although there is less evidence of personal expertise in some areas, the author's chapter on how the pharmaceutical industry has a hold on the NHS goes over much well-rehearsed ground in an engaging way. Again there is the familiar shadow of that other author in this field: Ivan Illich's Medical Nemesis comes to mind. Similarly, he discusses the very many conspiracy theories around the death of John F Kennedy, the less well-rehearsed but equally suspicious theories around the 'suicide' of Dr. David Kelly and, perhaps less authoritatively, the belief that Hitler survived and lived in Argentina after the Second World War. But perhaps most intriguingly is his chapter concerning UFOs. He manages to bring together the testimonies of many of those who have reported sightings. On top of that he writes that he has personally spoken to a number of astronauts whose accounts to do with the Moon landings lead him to believe with others that no landings have actually ever taken place.

The *Conspiracy Conspiracy* is not an attempt to resurrect the despicable hoax 'The Protocols of the Elders of Zion' which purported to describe an imagined meeting of leading Jews who planned to take over the world in a secret conspiracy. Instead David Bryant asks if those in power collude in fooling the public in many areas of life to their own ends. He points to the power that the Rothermere press and Rupert Murdoch's publications have in informing (or misinforming) the British public. However, the fact that they usually give the same slant to any story probably means that they share the same world view and the same self interests. The fact that David Bryant, Ivan Illich and I share the same view of the education system does not mean we have conspired – we probably just share the same world view. Readers of this book who also share the same world view as the author will find the book hard to put down. But the author would probably most welcome those of a more sceptical persuasion – just as he has always been.

Ray Kohn 2018

THE CONSPIRACY CONSPIRACY

Introduction

WHAT is a conspiracy? Put simply, it's two or more people operating together towards a common goal: one criminal might plan and carry out a bank raid or rob a mail train, two or more might be accused of 'conspiracy to commit a felony'. Our modern understanding of the word also carries with it the idea of a group of individuals involved in a clandestine operation to carry out a subversive or illegal act in order to achieve political or financial goals, who then attempt to hide the evidence that they are doing so until their plans are successful. For example, 'Valkerie', the plot to assassinate Adolf Hitler, was a conspiracy carried out by a large group of high-ranking Nazi officers, while, supposedly, the Gunpowder plot of 1605 was a similar undertaking by British Catholics to destroy the English King James 1st and his parliament.

I have been studying the 'conspiracy phenomenon' for as long as I have been aware of it: that's to say for around forty years. I first began to realize that things were not always as they are reported or recorded in history books in November 1963.

Even to a twelve year old boy, the assassination of President John Kennedy in Dealey Plaza and the astonishing speed

THE CONSPIRACY CONSPIRACY

with which his alleged murderer was first captured and then rapidly 'dealt with' by a local night-club owner, seemed more like a Hollywood film script than reality. I closely followed the deliberations of the Warren Commission and read every book and magazine article I could get hold of: this interest in the career of JFK and his family continues to intrigue me today. The Bay of Pigs, the Cuba missile Crisis, Marilyn Monroe's 'suicide', the assassination of Robert Kennedy and Martin Luther King, Teddy Kennedy and the shameful events at Chappaquidick – even, perhaps, the death of John Kennedy Junior – seem stranger and less transparent the more closely they're examined.

Although the phrase 'Conspiracy Theory' has been in use since the nineteenth century, it has been widely suggested that it was first deployed in a derogatory manner by the CIA in the 1960s to discredit the ideas of those who questioned the official account of the assassination of JFK and the report of the Warren Commission.

For many years I ran a very profitable business selling items associated with the exploration of space: these included flown artefacts from German, US and Russian launch vehicles and spacecraft as well as books, photographs and other ephemera signed by test pilots and astronauts. During the fifteen years or so that I ran 'The Space Station' (as the business was called) I frequently had the opportunity to meet many famous Russian Cosmonauts and US Astronauts. Despite my admiration – then and now – for these courageous men and women, I gradually became aware of a number of serious contradictions in many of their accounts. Whenever the opportunity arose, I discussed my thoughts with other spaceflight enthusiasts: the more critically I examined the Apollo lunar missions, the more I was forced to conclude that the accepted history was based upon a carefully designed program of disinformation and manipulation that can only have originated at the highest levels of government and the NASA administration.

I recall an old saying that my Scottish grandfather occasionally used:

'How do you know your father is your father? Because your mother told you so!'

It began to occur to me that the same sort of unquestioning acceptance underpinned many other historical 'truths'. Just because a scientist or politician states something as a fact, that doesn't make it so, and yet most people never doubt the word of the experts they have been programmed to trust! If you *really* wished to discover whether the man you've called 'Dad' your whole life really is your genetic father, the only course of action would be to have several independent DNA tests carried out. Of course, validating some of history's more contentious events would be somewhat more problematical. Take the Apollo 'Conspiracy', for example. Even if the US, Russia, China or anyone else were to land astronauts on the Moon in the future and visit the six landing sites, how could you be certain that the Lunar Module bases, various bits of

THE CONSPIRACY CONSPIRACY

hardware and three Lunar Rovers had been there for fifty or so years?

Cast-iron proof should **already** exist that these items are on the lunar surface, but it doesn't! A very highly-placed individual involved in the operation of the SR71 'Blackbird' once informed me that – even through fifteen or more miles of moisture-laden atmosphere – this astonishing surveillance aircraft could image objects just a few centimetres long! Given the advances in camera and computer technology, he continued, he was surprised that the pictures captured by the cameras of the Lunar Reconnaissance Orbiter in 2012 were of such poor quality, especially taking into account the Moon's total lack of atmosphere. He reckoned you should be able to count the ridges in Buzz Aldrin's footprints!

It was during my research into the Apollo program that I first came across the pejorative use of the phrase 'Conspiracy Theorist': this has increasingly become the case, so that today it is almost a synonym for 'credulous crackpot'! Whenever someone expresses an opinion at odds with the mainstream historical record, the default response is to label them as a 'Conspiracy Theorist', holding them up to ridicule and dismissal out of hand.

At first I didn't see this as part of a wider hidden agenda: but, following the publication of a couple of my books, various postings on my 'Chilling Tales UK' website and several years of public lectures about the alleged Moon landings and the UFO phenomenon, I started to consider the idea that the

THE CONSPIRACY CONSPIRACY

deployment of the phrase and concept 'Conspiracy Theory' was part of a carefully considered strategy. It seemed to me that labelling any new thinking about a contentious issue as part of a 'Conspiracy Theory' was a great way of hiding some genuine but inconvenient truths among a rag-bag collection of urban legends, myths and fantasies.

As an example of this, consider the fact that TV programmes about UFOs, are, in the UK at least, often presented by celebrities from unrelated areas of entertainment (Danny Dyer, Shaun Ryder, Clive Anderson and Mark Williams, for example) and frequently form part of a series of far less credible topics which are easily dismissed or ridiculed. These might include the 'The ancestors of the British Royal Family and other ruling elites were reptilian aliens', 'Sodom and Gomorrah were destroyed in an ancient nuclear conflict' or 'Flight 19 disappeared without explanation in the mysterious Bermuda Triangle'.

Now whereas it might be quite reasonable to examine the way in which the world's wealth resides in the bank accounts of a very few obscenely rich family dynasties (and some Russian oligarchs!), the belief that this is because their ancestries can be traced back to an ancient ruling elite of lizard-like aliens is a little more difficult to sustain. The result is that the average viewer, encouraged by the jokey, genial tones of a 'Fast Show' comedian, may well bundle together the UFO phenomenon with 'Did aliens build Stonehenge?' It's a little like having highlights of the Northern Ballet dancing

THE CONSPIRACY CONSPIRACY

Swan Lake on Match of the Day and asking Alan Shearer to analyse their performance!

Assuming for a moment that genuine conspiracies **are** usually reported in a dismissively light-hearted way, does that prove the existence of a 'conspiracy conspiracy' – a conscious attempt to bury inconvenient truths in a morass of ludicrous conjecture? We need to consider the part played by the media in forming public opinion and who defines that role...

For far longer than you might imagine, politicians, dictators and other ruling elites have fully understood this basic principle: if you control what people hear, see and read, you control what they believe! If you can also erode people's analytical powers, and make them virtually uncritical, so much the better. It is an astonishing fact that less than twenty individuals own and control the mass media of the western world: in the UK, recently published figures indicate that just three companies control 70% of national newspapers while five publish 80% of local titles. This puts the power to influence public opinion in the hands of a small cabal of unelected individuals, some of whom also control radio, TV and cable concerns.

Linguist and Political theorist Naom Chomsky has produced an exceptional analysis of this process in action, called 'Ten Strategies for Manipulation':

"The quality of education given to the lower social classes must be as poor and mediocre as possible, so

that the gap of ignorance (between) the lower classes and upper classes is, and remains, impossible for the lower classes to bridge."

Chomsky goes on to assert that the process is continued by developing 'complacence in mediocrity' If you can brainwash adolescents into thinking that ignorance, mediocrity and vulgarity are in fact mature, fashionable and sophisticated, you erode their powers of critical thought. They may well carry these behaviours into adulthood or adults may themselves adopt them in order to present a youthful image. In either case, the end result is a population that sees no value in traditional beliefs or behaviours and which promotes new ideals like the importance of wealth, possession, status and appearance. What we have ended up with in the west is a generation who expect fame, fortune and beauty without having to work too hard for any of it: hence the rise of talent shows, botox, lotteries and online gambling.

All of this, of course, distracts the population from a critical understanding of how they are being manipulated to protect the status quo of the ruling elites. For example: how many young people (or old ones for that matter!) have ever really thought about the three immoral and probably illegal wars in which the UK has been involved in recent decades. The long-awaited Chilcot enquiry, with its damning indictment of Tony Blair and his advisors, went largely unreported: certainly it slipped beneath the radar of the majority of the British population. I would suggest that this is the result of long-term strategic manipulation of society, its members and the rules by which they live.

If you can successfully foster a culture driven by consumerism and egocentricity and which places little or no value on history, respect for tradition and empathy for others, you are in a strong position to make use of the most effective tool for the control of any society:

Problem: Reaction: Solution

Many people assume that this political strategy was first exposed and defined by author and broadcaster David Icke in his books and lectures, but in fact its origins are generally conceded to lie in the writings of Georg Wilhelm Friedrich Hegel.

In the nineteenth century, German philosopher Heinrich Moritz Chalybäus defined the Hegelian Dialectic in terms of three phases:

A ***thesis***, giving rise to a reaction, followed by an ***antithesis*** or contrary response to this, leading to a resolution of this conflict by means of a ***synthesis***.

This concept was discussed and developed into the principle of Dialectical Materialism by political theorists Marx and Engels, eventually forming the basis for revolutionary writings by Lenin, Stalin and Mao.

As I will reveal again and again, this has become the default strategy of politicians and leaders throughout history: they will claim to have identified a threat (real or imaginary) to the proletariat, wait for a public reaction and then suggest a course of action that not only resolves the initial problem but also allows for further control of the population. If this seems to have little to do with modern life, here are a few brief examples:

Problem: Dangers of cigarette smoking.

Reaction: Fear of illness caused by personal or secondary inhalation.

Solution: Raised tobacco prices, ban on public smoking, demonization of all forms of tobacco use.

Additional outcomes: A steady increase in the revenues from tobacco taxation, the rise of the 'Vaping' industry, smuggling and, possibly, increased use of other recreational drugs.

Problem: The threat of international terrorism.

Reaction: Fear, leading to a demand for greater security.

Solution: Increased surveillance and covert action.

Additional planned outcomes: armed police and military personnel on the streets, routine eaves-dropping on e-mail, social media and phone conversations. Demonization of ethnic/religious groups: military action overseas.

THE CONSPIRACY CONSPIRACY

Problem: Air pollution in cities.

Reaction: Fear of lung disease caused by car exhaust.

Solution: Emission and congestion charges and fines: promotion of cycling and electrical vehicles.

Additional planned outcomes: Increased tax revenues, public transport over-stretched, small transport and courier firms driven out of business, conflict between cyclists, pedestrians and motorists, expanded sales opportunities for manufacturers of electric cars. Inner city house prices are no longer affordable by ordinary people, resulting in property speculation and green belt development outside cities.

Problem: Plastic pollution.

Reaction: Fear that the Earth's seas/ecosystems will collapse.

Solution: A tax on takeaway coffee cups and ban on free carrier bags.

Additional planned outcomes: Extra revenue for government, coffee bars and supermarkets, which continue to provide carrier bags for 3p each and 'bags for life' at an increased price.

At one time my business interests took me (and my commercial vehicle!) inside the emission zone twice a year. I couldn't afford to have my van uprated or buy a replacement:

THE CONSPIRACY CONSPIRACY

to my amazement I found I could still enter the zone by paying a daily tariff of £100! In other words: the emission charge could seem to have more to do with making money than protecting the lungs of Londoners!

In conclusion, this book is intended as an attempt to encourage its readers to think more deeply about how and why we respond to the frequent – and often conflicting – pronouncements of the many experts who affect and regulate all of our lives.

In each chapter, I'll examine some of the modern sacred cows of institutionalized belief and consider to what extent they are subverted to manipulate public opinion and attitudes – and why! I will use examples from my own experiences where possible: at least *I* can be certain these are true!

Throughout, I will highlight how the default pejorative phrase 'conspiracy theory' is intentionally used by the media, politicians and lobbyists for political and financial advantage and to hide a number of serious issues that affect us all.

A final thought: given the proliferation of Kindle-style book downloads, closure of public libraries and disappearance of book shops from the high street, you might legitimately ask whether there will be a demand for printed books such as this in the future. (My personal belief is that there is unlikely to be a mass audience, but that there will always be a few people who enjoy handling and owning 'real' books.)

Could the marginalization of the printed word be another example of 'dumbing down' of the population?

THE CONSPIRACY CONSPIRACY

Chapter 1: A spoonful of sugar?

IN 2011 I reached sixty years of age. Unquestionably I was overweight, unquestionably I drank too much wine. On the other hand, I'd been a vegetarian for thirty years and ate little or no sugar in the form of sweets, biscuits or puddings. A routine visit to the doctor's surgery for a 'well man check' resulted in a diagnosis of type 2 diabetes. This, of course, was very worrying! I attended a few discussion groups and researched the condition on line, before deciding on an all-out frontal attack on the underlying causes of the disease. I stopped drinking alcohol, cut my daily consumption of bread to two slices and began walking five or more miles every day. I also bought a home sugar testing kit. Within a year I had lost over four stones and, according to the testing kit, was now well in the normal blood sugar range. All well and good, except I eventually discovered that every 60+ year-old male I knew had also received the same 'pre-diabetic' diagnosis. Many of them (unwilling or unable to make dramatic life-style changes) had progressed to daily doses of *metformin* and DPP-4 inhibitors. What I found interesting was that a number of these individuals were comparatively slim and barely drank any alcohol. The received wisdom is, of course,

THE CONSPIRACY CONSPIRACY

that the major causes of type 2 diabetes are weight and bad diet.

In 2015, it was reported that there were 360 million people around the world living with type 2 diabetes. Interestingly, certain racial types display a predisposition: in the USA, for example, the condition is more common among Native Americans, Hispanics and Asian Americans.

I began to wonder whether or not there might be a hidden agenda here somewhere... It occurred to me that, perhaps, type 2 diabetes is actually the **normal condition** of men (and to a lesser extent, women) over the age of sixty. My reasons for thinking this were:

- There seems to be a strong genetic component (the propensity, to some extent, appears to run in families)
- There is an apparent racial bias
- It is definitely linked to reduced activity and weight increase.
- It is definitely linked to old age

Here's a thought! Human beings are now living well beyond their sell-by dates: both men and women reach their peaks of sexual fertility in their early thirties: in both there is a sharp decline after forty. In other words we are biologically redundant by middle age, just like all the other primates on Earth. (Ever looked at film of an old silver-backed Gorilla? They're not exactly slim, are they?)

When I visit my GP for an annual check up, I can be certain

that he will tell me that I am clinically obese: this despite having shed over 25 kilos since I turned 60. Occasionally I ask him which definition he is applying: of course, the reply is the BMI (body mass index)

This method of classifying the human race into normal, overweight and obese groups using the ratio between mass and height squared, was first suggested in 1972 as a system for comparing **populations** rather than **individuals**. The coloured graphs your doctor refers to when he is encouraging you to lose weight are, it should be remembered, entirely arbitrary. At some point a 'panel of experts' at the World Health Organisation metaphorically sat around a table and decided on the cut-off points for each group.

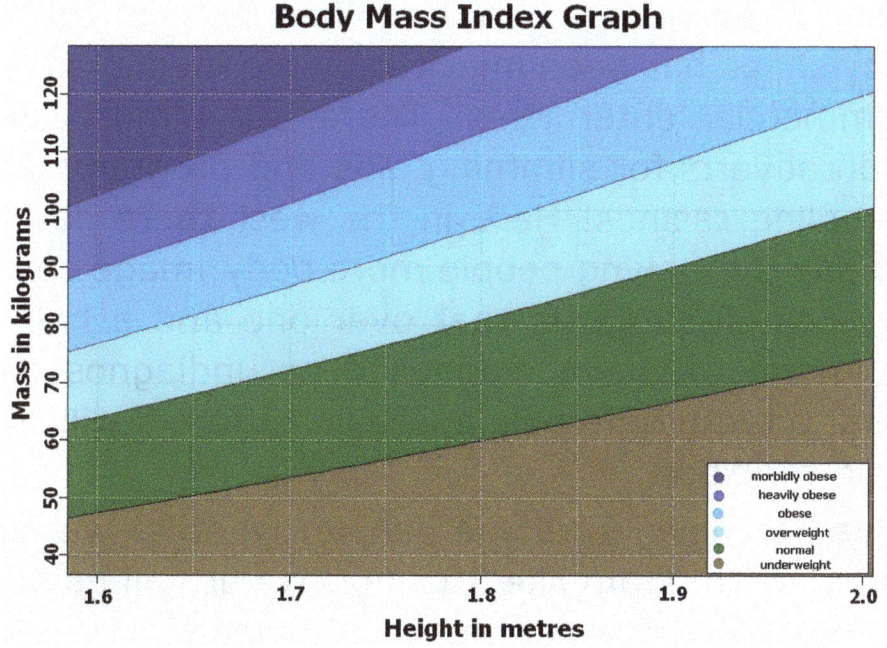

Plate 1: Body Mass Index

THE CONSPIRACY CONSPIRACY

Now, in late middle age both my parents became heavier, as did my older brother: this seems to be the case with most of my acquaintances, with the exception of a few who can eat whatever they like and remain skinny. Doctors are very busy people these days, but occasionally I have had the opportunity to discuss this with my GP: under pressure – or just, perhaps, to get rid of me – he eventually conceded that the BMI is by and large an arbitrary construct which fails to take into account age, genetic propensity or racial type. Intriguingly, studies published in 2014 by researchers in a number of countries strongly indicate that a higher BMI may actually ***increase*** the life span of older people!

Of course, it is entirely appropriate for the medical profession to encourage healthier lifestyles, but this stereotyping by shape has been hijacked by the media, advertising and commercial enterprises. There are almost as many television adverts for slimming aids and programs as there are for online casinos! Here in the west there has been a price to pay for making people more body-image conscious: recent research suggests that over one and a half million people in the UK have diagnosed or undiagnosed eating disorders: a tenth of female anorexia sufferers will currently die of the condition.

I have bad news for some people: whether we, doctors, politicians or film stars like it or not, we are all going to get old and die! Now most of us live in houses and obtain our food from the supermarket (rather than chasing it around

THE CONSPIRACY CONSPIRACY

the landscape) Getting old has therefore generally resulted in reduced mobility, weight gain and gradual physical decline. Of course, in the modern world, we humans are expected to conform to some pretty challenging stereotypes: both men and women are prepared to put themselves through a lot to look younger than they really are: perpetual diets, daily gym sessions, jogging and hair colour are pretty standard. For men there is an additional problem: even after production of the male hormone testosterone slows down, they continue to produce the 'female' hormone oestrogen. After the age of thirty, testosterone levels decrease by 1% annually, so that many men undergo a 'male menopause', resulting in sexual dysfunction, breast enlargement and weight gain. What's one of the most common surgical procedures in the USA? Male breast reduction! Now while Hormone Replacement Therapy is fairly routinely prescribed for women, this is not the case for men! I once asked my GP why this should be: his reply was that the link between testosterone and aggression makes it potentially too dangerous.

I'd bet if you're a tubby gent of fifty-plus, your GP has already suggested you might be on the threshold of type 2 diabetes. In many parts of the UK, you will have been invited to take part in a 'diabetes study' which involves you regularly visiting a clinic at your local hospital or health centre for blood tests and group discussion. And yet, to be frank, what will probably see you off will be one or a combination of the top five killers:

THE CONSPIRACY CONSPIRACY

Dementia
Cancer
Stroke
Heart disease
Lung disease

Our wild ancestors certainly didn't live long enough to worry about any of these: the palaeolithic top five was probably:

Predation by wild animals
Illness (microbial infection/parasite infestation)
Poisoning
Injury
Starvation

Most of these are no longer an issue in civilized society, and warfare (unless someone pushes the red button) is responsible for surprisingly few deaths globally, despite what you might imagine from watching the six o'clock news! This is, of course, why the population of the planet is growing so alarmingly: it may well be that competition for food, water and somewhere to live may re-enter the equation fairly soon.

Various Government agencies periodically release figures to demonstrate that life expectancy – the maximum age (based on national averages) that a newborn child could be anticipated to reach – is steadily increasing as a result of improvements in living conditions, diet and health initiatives.

It is conceded that this data reveals considerable variation depending on where you happen to live (bad news if you're Scottish, good news if you were born in Chelsea!) and that the rate of increase has shown signs of slowing down. However, reading through the redacted figures published in the popular press, you might come to believe that politicians have altruistically done a wonderful job of helping us live longer than our parents. But is this actually the case?

Take a walk around any old cemetery: although the gravestones reveal the dreadful extent of infant mortality a century ago, you'll notice that plenty of people lived to 80 or 90 years of age. This is the first reason why modern statistics demonstrate higher life expectancy: the infant mortality rate is far lower. Despite eating all the wrong foods, smoking like chimneys and living in insanitary, overcrowded squalor, if you remove the child deaths from the equation, you find that adult life expectancy hasn't changed that much in a hundred years. Since the 1980s the IMR in the UK has dropped by over 60%, to just 3.6 deaths per thousand births: at the end of the nineteenth century it was 150 per thousand live births!

Another really significant factor is the improvement in medical and surgical procedures: once fatal conditions such as cardiac arrest, severe burns and bacterial diseases are now treatable with antibiotics, better antiseptics and new surgical techniques. In other words, little or none of the rise in life expectancy is actually associated with increasing our

potential life span: this is the same now as it was ten thousand years ago! Avoiding all illness, injury, accidents and eating a balanced, nutritious diet, the majority of us will live to 80 or 90 and then die of 'old age'. Let's undertake a brief consideration of why this happens.

Our body is made up of around 60 trillion individual living units called cells: thousands of different varieties carrying out all the functions needed to keep us alive. The different types of cell have finite life spans: this varies from 39 days in the case of epithelial skin cells to ten years or more for bone cells.

Without getting too deeply into the science of genetics, most people are aware that every cell in the human body (apart from red blood cells!) contains a structure called the nucleus. This controls the cell's functions and also contains complex arrangements of organic molecules called nucleic acids. In most cases these are contained within the **nucleus**, on dark rod-like structures known as **chromosomes**: discrete regions of these carry 'chemical instructions' that control one or more individual functions: these are called **genes**.

The method by which our cells reproduce during growth, repair or replacement is by a process called mitosis: this is also the way that simple organisms such as the familiar Amoeba reproduce.

Of course, this possibility is not available to animals with high levels of organisation: if a cat were split into two, both

THE CONSPIRACY CONSPIRACY

halves (lacking the necessary life-support structures) would die. This form of cell reproduction is how complex organisms like humans grow and repair damaged tissue: the essential feature being the copying and passing on of the parent-cell's full genetic 'blueprint' during the process of **transcription.**

If you've ever used a photo-copier, you'll be aware that each time you copy a document there is some degradation in quality. If you copied a photo-copy, then copied **that**, and continued to do so a dozen times, the end result would be blurred and incomplete. There are *always* mistakes in the chromosome transcription process, but the cell's repair system corrects them. As we grow older, however, this gradually performs less efficiently: after a lifetime's division, cells may be produced that are less able to carry out their function. In other words, growing old and dying appear to be related to the increasing inability of the body to regenerate new, efficient cells: it's almost as if evolution has generated built in redundancy into all living things.

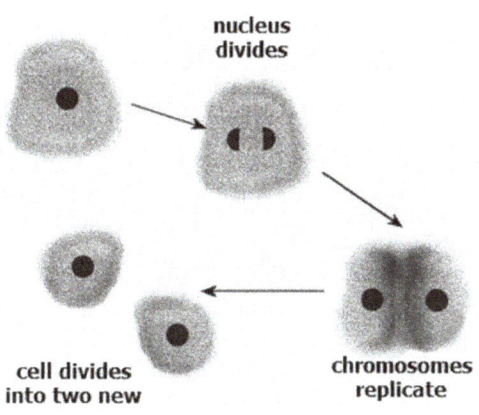

Plate2: Mitosis

No matter what any of us do – or don't do – we are all biologically fated to wear out and die: all we can attempt to do is attempt to live a long, productive life with as few serious injuries and illnesses as possible along the way.

THE CONSPIRACY CONSPIRACY

So why do doctors, scientists and politicians continue to alarm us with the threat of new and dreadful pandemics? Well I can think of a few reasons: sixteen billion in fact! In 2015, that was the amount the NHS spent on drugs alone! Who benefits from continually promoting the use of new medicines? The obvious answer is, of course, the people who manufacture and sell them. If a drug company can come up with something vaguely innovative and vaguely therapeutic, and can persuade the NHS to adopt it, they have a licence to print money until the next big thing comes along. Human nature being what it is, it would be surprising if a few medical or political palms were not oiled to ensure the adoption and prescription of the new drug. If you can invent a new illness for your wonder drug to treat, so much the better!

In recent years we have all been scared to death by media hype about some new disease that is going to sweep across the globe like Asian flu and kill us in our millions. Remember Swine Flu? Bird Flu? SARS? Ebola? Creutzfeldt Jakob disease? Possibly not, since all of these turned out to be damp squibs, killing fewer people globally than road traffic accidents.

Millions are spent annually on flu vaccines, yet Sir Macfarlane Burnet, Nobel laureate, and leading authority on influenza viruses once observed:

"**A vaccine .... reduces the risk of catching flu only by half. This hardly measures up to our expectations for a modern vaccine. Furthermore, the remarkable** *propensity of influenza to undergo antigenic drift ensures that in any major new pandemic, the virus will always be one step ahead of the manufacturers."*

Some years back, predicted epidemics of Swine and Bird Flu failed to materialise, but not before the NHS had been persuaded to stock pile vast numbers of doses of vaccine of doubtful efficacy but of **known** potential risk. Not much thought is required to work out who might have benefitted from this decision.

A little personal anecdote! A few years ago, because I am a) old and b) at risk (having a history of T2 Diabetes) I was given a once-in-a-lifetime pneumococcal polysaccharide vaccination (PPV) against pneumonia. This 'jab' costs the NHS between £40 and £70 a shot. Five years after I had mine, I contracted double pneumonia (winter bird watching, I'm afraid!) and came very close to checking out: so much for therapeutic precautionary immunisation!

Do you see echoes in all this of **'problem: reaction: solution'**? It certainly seems as if the regular discovery of a 'new' disease is generally followed by widespread public panic (often exacerbated up by the tabloid press). This in turn leads to the announcement of a vaccine by our heroic health minister and his team, for which we are all so pitifully grateful that we fail to observe that no-one is actually getting ill and – more significantly – that some people are getting wealthy! Generally some element of control or modification of our behaviour is involved too.

THE CONSPIRACY CONSPIRACY

Let's now turn our attention to a different type of drug: the sort you don't get from the doctor! Another anecdote: I'm full of them!

After leaving school, I became a Helicopter Pilot cadet in the Royal Navy.

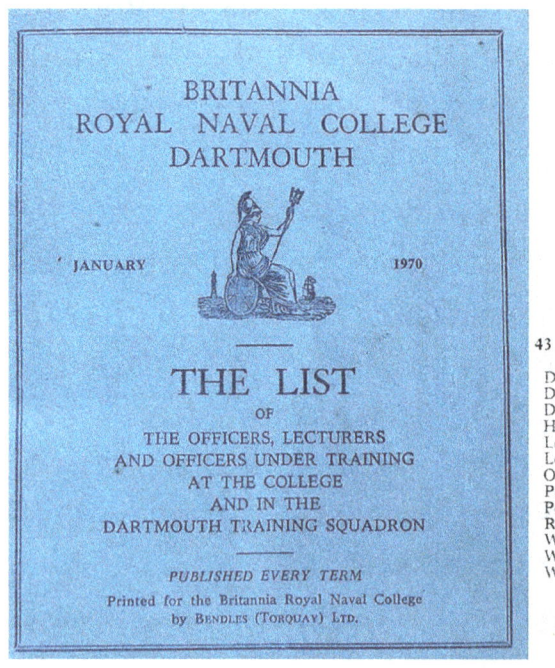

Plate 3: Navy list

During my time at Dartmouth I fell ill and spent a week or so in the medical facility at the College. Before I returned to duty, the Surgeon Captain in charge of the unit sat me down for a little chat, during which he observed that I habitually 'jogged' my legs up and down (still do, as a matter of fact!).

"You're a bag of nerves, Cadet... Do you smoke?"

"Nossir!"

"Well when you return to your division, tell the Div CPO that you wish to declare yourself as a smoker – it'll calm you down a bit and help your flying!"

This I duly did: at the next pay parade I presented my pay book with the smokers' chit and received a sheet of cigarette vouchers. These I redeemed at the NAAFI for 400 'blue liners' which cost me 10p for the lot! Within a few days I was a committed smoker: a habit from which I finally escaped twenty years later. Then, and for some years afterwards, the general consensus was that smoking was a useful aid to concentration, suppressing the appetite and maintaining levels of alertness. I recall that at every break during route marches and 'yomps' across Dartmoor our Marine instructors always shouted out:

'*Those who smoke, smoke: those who don't, go through the motions!*'

Forty year ago, smoking was the rule rather than the exception. The staffroom at the first school at which I taught was perpetually shrouded in pipe smoke: many of the Science staff habitually fired up their briers in the 'prep. rooms' at the back of their laboratories and it was customary for staff to enjoy a cigarette while on playground duty.

How and why did all this change? It's not as if it hadn't been known for donkey's years that there was a causative link between smoking, lung disease and premature death.

What we're looking at here is, I believe, the first major muscle-flexing of the 'nanny state'. The fairly rapid persecu-

THE CONSPIRACY CONSPIRACY

tion of smokers was almost without precedent: those with the habit found it more and more difficult to enjoy a cigarette and increasingly expensive to do so. When I first smoked back in 1970, a pack of 20 Rothmans cost around 20p: the modern unlabelled equivalent retails at close to £8 at the time of writing!

It is generally stated that the reason for the increased strictures on a habit that even members of the Royal Family used to enjoy (and die from!) was intended to reduce the pressure on the National Health Service: but I can see a paradox here...

If more people smoked, they'd die younger and therefore not live into old age to clutter up care homes, hospitals and surgeries.

Their houses would become available for recycling much more quickly.

Their jobs would become available sooner, alleviating unemployment.

Dying younger, they'd draw their state pension for a much shorter period. In any case, tobacco revenues have always been a significant fraction of the UK's tax receipts, some of which must end up in the NHS where it necessarily contributes towards treatment of people with smoking-related illnesses.

Don't get the idea I'm an apologist for smoking: it was – and continues to be – a filthy habit. I'm delighted that I can enjoy a meal in a restaurant without having to suck up other people's tobacco fumes or visit the theatre without smelling

THE CONSPIRACY CONSPIRACY

like an ashtray when I leave. But my question is this: why not just ban smoking/vaping altogether? It's almost as if various governments have been aware that hiding cigarettes behind an opaque screen in the supermarket and decorating the packets with gruesome images and warnings actually lends them a certain dangerous rebel *cachet*, somewhat along the lines of riding a motorbike in jeans and a tee-shirt.

A cynic might suspect that the current measures make it **seem** as if the government is acting to promote a healthy life while still benefitting from tobacco revenues.

In 2016 there were still nearly eight million smokers in the UK plus a further three million 'vapers' who between them generated 12 billion pounds in tax revenue in that year. (This is around a tenth of the total NHS budget.) The UK is still a major exporter of tobacco products, although the value of this trade is very hard to discover online. The revenue from this trade is certainly significant: US export analysts put the volume of UK exports at **forty five billion cigarettes** per year.

You have to ask the question: does any government have the **right** to dictate to the people it **serves** what and how much they can consume? Surely their role is only advisory: they should present incontrovertible data and encourage people to make choices based upon this. You may remember how past Ministers of Health have tried to persuade us that butter, cheese, eggs, chicken, red meat and even milk are bad for us!

Next on the shopping list could easily be alcohol, of course: but here the politicians have a real problem: the value of the UK drinks trade is around sixty billion pounds annually. That is a huge sum to write off!

There are any number of examples of government health policy being based around faulty data or theories: back in the fifties, for example, it was routine for children to have their tonsils and adenoids surgically removed: now it is recognised that both play a significant role in the body's immune system, producing and storing the white blood cells that help combat microbial infection.

Many people have suggested that the overuse of antibiotics, immunisation and obsessive hygiene have all contributed towards a decline in our ability to fight infection. When I was a young boy it was customary for parents to encourage their children to socialise with others who were suffering from measles, chicken pox or German measles so that they could either develop immunity to these diseases or catch them and get them 'out of the way' before they started school. This 'herd immunity' meant that many youngsters reached adulthood with acquired resistance to illnesses like mumps and shingles that are far more debilitating in later life. These days things are a lot different: parents are 'encouraged' to have their babies immunised with the following:

Pneumococcal jab (PCV)
Hib/Men C vaccine
MMR vaccine

THE CONSPIRACY CONSPIRACY

6-in-1 vaccine
Children's flu vaccine
4-in-1 pre-school booster
HPV vaccine (girls only)
3-in-1 teenage booster

Various opponents of this policy have expressed concerns about possible side effects of some or all of these, including autism, bowel disease and ITP (bleeding under the skin). Generally, their research is ridiculed, marginalised and suppressed: the careers of a number of notable paediatricians have been destroyed in this way.

A few years ago I came across a good example of how unquestioning compliance with government health guidelines can border on the ludicrous. During the Swine Flu 'pandemic' of 2009 (which incidentally resulted in less than 250 deaths worldwide!) all hospitals, clinics, GP surgeries and many public buildings were equipped with hand disinfectant stations by their entrance doors: the cost to the NHS (and the profits earned by the manufacturers) must have been incredible. I pointed out to the receptionists and my GP that the waiting room was full of newspapers, magazines and handouts that had been there for many months. These had undoubtedly been handled by thousands of patients, many suffering from infectious diseases! These were removed before my next visit, at which time I added that soft furnishings, clothes, hair, shoes, handbags (and the books people were bringing in to read in the absence of magazines!) were as likely vectors of infection as their hands: these, after all, are customarily washed far more frequently than any other part of the human body. Soon after the disinfectant stations disappeared!

A few years ago I had serious thoracic surgery: this necessitated a couple of weeks in the ICU. I was in a side ward with five other men of similar age: one by one these became ill with MRSA and began to die. Astonishingly, the survivors (including yours truly, of course!) were sent home early: one of them (a WW2 Lancaster pilot) actually went home in a taxi **with a drip stand and drip!**

Soon after, this ancient and insanitary hospital was replaced by a brand spanking new one, which really is one of the best in the UK.

During my spell of hospital-time there (following the pneumonia I mentioned earlier) I waited on a trolley for a number of hours before a bed became available. (I want to state here and now that I offer **no criticism** of the nurses, doctors and support staff at the hospital: they did an incredible job and it's no exaggeration to say I owe my life to them.) During my brief stay I was moved twice: the consultant who was treating me confided that many of the wards were over capacity, largely because of the number of dementia patients with nowhere else to go.

It was almost impossible to sleep because of the behaviour of many of these poor people. After four nights I was quietly informed that if I could walk to the toilet and back I might be released early. Despite profound weakness, lack of energy and dizziness, I struggled to the bathroom at four the following morning. I shaved, washed my hair and went to the loo: this took me an hour and a half! The result was that I was back home in time for my birthday two days later (although I was pretty ill for many weeks afterwards).

Given these two examples from my own experience, you'd have to conclude that however much money the government throws at the NHS it is unlikely that there will ever be enough hospital beds, doctors, nurses and infrastructure, simply because we are all living way beyond expectations! The problem of accommodating dementia sufferers has been exacerbated by the closure of scores of Cottage Hospitals across the UK and the disappearance of the traditional extended family. Only a concerted effort to discover the causes and methods of prevention of this terrible illness would improve things.

What is true in medicine and surgery is even more the case in dentistry: have you managed to find an NHS practice that has room for you? My excellent NHS dentist was bought out by foreign investors and immediately became a private practice. After much searching, we were accepted by another surgery, where a dentist from Hungary – who had a somewhat sketchy command of English – removed a perfectly healthy tooth by mistake while replacing a crown (which she also removed!).

My wife and I now use an excellent private practice: the sole practitioner has all the best equipment and skills to match, but we could have bought a car (honestly!) with what we have spent with him in the past ten years.

Given the inarguable and unsustainable pressure on the health service and welfare state in general, does it make any sense to prolong people's lives **regardless of their own thoughts on the subject** or capacity to enjoy their final years?

I have personal experience of the suffering that may result from prolonging a person's life well beyond their capacity to enjoy it. My mother developed Multiple Sclerosis in late middle age: at first it was merely an inconvenience to her, but fairly rapidly she was confined to a wheelchair. At this point I helped her move from the outskirts of London to half a mile from my house in Norfolk. This meant my wife and I could visit her daily and, being a very outgoing and gregarious person, she quickly built up a circle of friends. Unfortunately her condition deteriorated rapidly until she required 24 hour nursing.

The last three years of her life were spent in a residential complex with incredibly high standards of care: she had her own four room apartment as well as excellent nursing staff and regular organised social events. But, of course, she was in constant pain and endured the frequent embarrassment associated with a total loss of bodily control.

While attempting to remain upbeat for her family's sake, she continually asked if there was some way of ending her suffering. In the end she took matters into her own hands and refused to eat: this certainly took more courage than I possess...

Who benefited from denying this proud and independent-minded lady a dignified death when she felt that her life was complete?

Conspiracy theory

The government's apparent promotion of healthier living and the alleged resultant longevity of the population is actually part of a cynical strategy:

- Increasing the retirement age for both men and women (justified by publishing over-optimistic figures of life expectancy) results in fewer survival years to draw state pensions. The ultimate goal is the complete cessation of the state 'Old Age Pension', with a substantial reduction in government outlay as the result.

- Keeping the population in work longer produces greater income tax and national insurance contributions. It also precludes the need to find something for active pensioners to do!

- Higher taxation of tobacco products generates revenue: the clever strategy of portraying smoking as dangerous and antisocial has been widely interpreted as indicative of a rebellious and devil-may-care attitude (rather than as a somewhat expensive working-class addiction) This has allowed the government to maintain the revenue stream while appearing to legislate against the habit.

- The same is true of alcohol taxation. If past governments were truly concerned about the social and physical effects of drinking alcohol, it's hard to see why they increased licensing hours and allowed the proliferation of 'buy one get one free offers in supermarkets.

- There is irrefutable proof linking the intelligence communities of western governments with the international drugs trade. Afghanistan has been the main supplier of Europe's heroin since the removal of the Taliban and remains such after their return.

- The apparent collapse of the National Health Service is actually a planned phasing out of free public healthcare, so that it can be replaced by compulsory individual private schemes.

- Tax paid by private care homes and wardened retirement communities generates significant income for the exchequer without any financial outlay.

Chapter 2: Education or indoctrination?

I feel I should start this section by admitting that (following my brief Navy career!) I was a teacher for over 35 years: 16 of them as Head of Environmental Sciences at a High School, 18 as Head of Key Stage 2 at a large primary school. Since leaving teaching I've spent fifteen years lecturing to adults and sixth form students. All of this, I'd like to feel, has given me a pretty complete personal insight into the UK education system and how it has changed in the past fifty years.

I was born just after the war on the edge of London's East End. My father – a genuine Cockney – was keen that my elder brother and I had every opportunity to 'get on in life', so he moved the family to Hornchurch, in metropolitan Essex. The school I attended was ancient and overcrowded: my school reports reveal class sizes of 50 to 60 and the staff (largely made up of elderly women) maintained discipline by the liberal use of the cane! Do I have happy memories of primary school? Not at all: even as a bit of a teacher's pet, I spent six years in silent fear of doing something punishable! However, by the time I left in 1962 I had a profound knowledge of the conventions of spelling, grammar and creative writing, and had instant recall of number bonds and tables up to 12 x 12 that have stayed with me my entire life (so far!) Of course, little Science was taught, there was no IT and Geography and History were basically 'Agriculture of the British Empire' and 'The Kings and Queens of England.' At the end of my time at North Street I took the 11+ exam, which I passed and was invited to follow my brother to the local Grammar School.

This potted history of my early life is not *just* an exercise in nostalgia but rather an opportunity to make comparisons with how things are done today.

The first and most obvious difference was that in the fifties, school was not intended to be fun! The main role of infant school was to institutionalise children: by the end of year two (age 6) pupils had learned to sit quietly and listen attentively. They were able to work independently and for quite long periods and accepted the necessity for good behaviour. There were no opportunities to leave the class for a drink or toilet break and no-one spoke unless invited to. This regime continued into Junior School: teachers were not friends or parent substitutes and you certainly didn't call them by their first names: they were 'Madam' or Sir'. No infringements of school or social rules were tolerated and any breaches were dealt with instantly.

By the end of my eighteen year spell in the management team of a primary school I was frequently frustrated by the ever-changing role of the classroom teacher and by the continually modified syllabuses they were compelled to deliver. The workloads of teachers in reception class were added to by the fact that increasing numbers of children arrived for their first day at school still wearing nappies and unable to use a knife and fork. Members of each new intake tended to have poor communication and interpersonal skills and often resented any attempt to modify their behaviour. By sheer hard work (and with an ever-increasing army of teaching assistants and ancillaries) the KS1 teachers usually managed to pre-format their charges by the time they moved up to Year 3. At this point, pupils attempted their first national written tests, the Key Stage 1 SATs, which had been rolled out in the UK between 1991 and 1995. Of course, since the introduction of the National Curriculum in 1988, teachers had been carrying out continual assessment from the start of each pupil's school career. (In passing: you might well wonder when any basic teaching was done, in between these assessments and the delivery of required non-core subjects, including, at various times, physical education, art, technology, religious knowledge, social studies and humanities.)

One of the buzz phrases in teaching back then (and probably now, too!) was 'value added': each year group had to demonstrate that **every** child had made progress during that year, regardless of socio-economic and ethnic backgrounds, personal and parental expectations and their own basic intelligence. No-one was allowed to fail or underachieve.

THE CONSPIRACY CONSPIRACY

I have no doubt that in a few schools, these expectations were fulfilled by manipulation of the KS1 SAT results: since these are marked and reported by the Class Teacher the potential (and opportunity) to massage end of key stage targets definitely exists. This, of course, makes it difficult for KS2 staff, will receive a new group in September with reported SAT results above their actual levels of attainment.

To sum up: it could be said that the nationally published primary SAT results are less meaningful than the old Eleven Plus exam. Since, in theory, they are not used to separate pupils into different education streams, what is their purpose? A moment's thought suggests that the SATS are there to check up on **teachers** rather than their pupils! Given the incredibly proscriptive nature and inflexible requirements of the National Curriculum and the vast volume of extra work imposed on teachers by marking, assessment and planning (strategic, tactical, operational and contingency), it's hardly surprising that morale and recruitment are at critical levels. I have mentored numbers of young teachers during their in-service training years who had indifferent degrees in subjects such as media studies, photography and performing arts. Others had previously been recruited from among the school's own teaching assistants, several of whom required tutoring to pass a GCSE in maths! Are standards – as we are continually told by successive governments – really rising? Or are we just lowering the bar?

Things are little better in the High Schools and Sixth

Form Colleges that replaced most Grammar Schools in 1976. Rigorous study and written examinations have largely been replaced by qualifications based on continuous assessment: this can contribute up to 60% of the marks in some subjects. For some years I was an examiner with the East Anglian Examination Board, being responsible for syllabuses and examinations for several CSE courses. (At the time CSE was intended to be attempted by around 40% of the sixteen year old pupils in English schools: the top 20% took the GCE examination, the remaining 40% left school with no academic qualifications.) Once all the papers had been marked, it was the panel's responsibility to set a grade curve. This involved establishing the pass mark for each exam and deciding what grade would be awarded for which marks. Suppose the pass mark is set at 50%: with a typical 'bell curve' distribution of marks achieved, as many candidates will pass as fail:

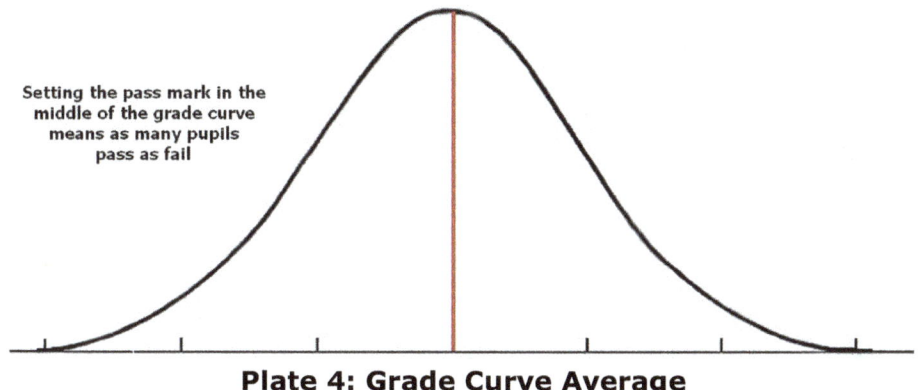

Plate 4: Grade Curve Average

During my time as an examiner, the grade curve was annually adjusted to maintain the same distribution of passes at each grade. This system can easily be manipulated by politicians to suggest that standards of achievement are improving: all that need be done is move the pass mark to the left, so that lower scores result in exam success:

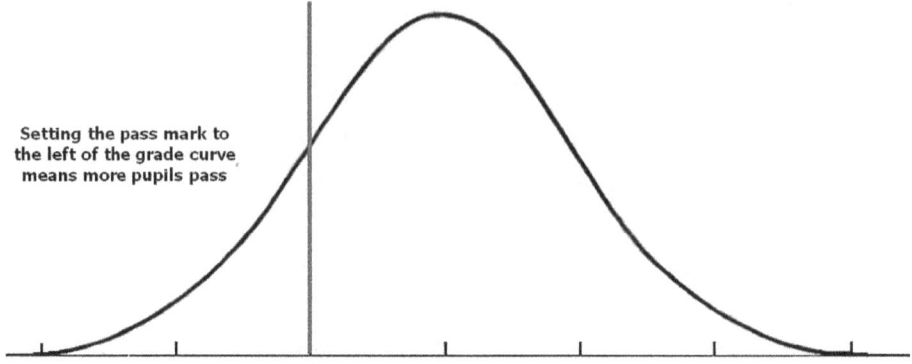

Plate 5: Grade Curve Higher Pass Rate

Similarly, the same results can be displayed to 'prove' that greater rigour is being applied to the setting of examinations and their marking:

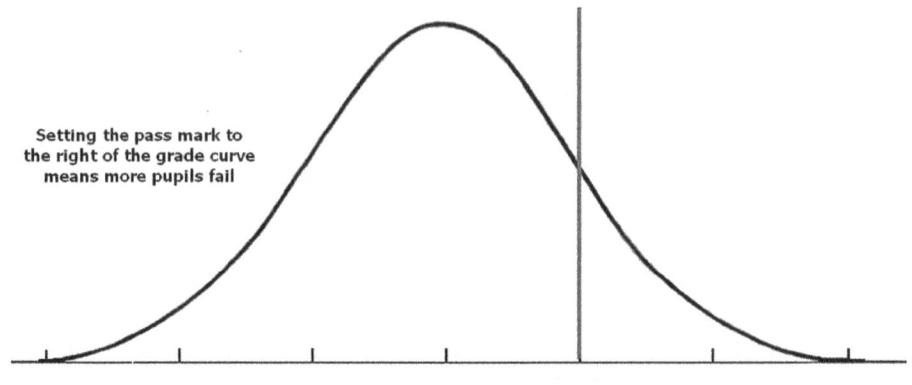

Plate 6: Grade Curve Lower Pass Rate

These three entirely different outcomes can be achieved with just *one* set of exam marks! Since the raw statistics are never made available, in this way the public can easily be fooled into believing that educational standards have been continually improved by the introduction of new government policies and regular modification of the National Curriculum and examination system. The graphs can be used to demonstrate the success of any government's policies or the shortcomings of their predecessors: they can 'prove' that standards are rising, or that teachers are failing in their responsibilities.

Since the lifetime of most governments is four years or less, this is a valuable tool for the party in power (and the opposition!) to use during the run-up to a general election.

In 1969 I left Grammar School with the required A and S levels and could have joined the elite 240,000 undergraduates at university: instead I chose to become a Naval Officer. Today, the figure is **ten times** this number! Does this indicate that there are now ten times as many bright school leavers each year? Logic suggests that the answer is no: rather, the entrance criteria are now less rigorous and many of the courses have been made less challenging. After all, if you can use the manipulation of public examinations to ensure a larger percentage achieves two or more A/S level passes, there won't be any problem increasing the University student population.

It could be said that giving every school leaver the opportunity to enter tertiary education can only be a good thing, but to what extent does a three year course in media studies or popular music equip a young person to make a productive contribution to modern society or help them achieve the standard of living they hope for? I can absolutely guarantee that captains of industry and commerce and front benchers of the major political parties are more likely to have studied traditional academic subjects such as economics.

So who benefits from such a large percentage of school leavers being encouraged to go into further education? (In 2017 30% of 18-year-olds were offered university places, while the figure for all higher education was close to 50%.)

To put it simply: while a teenager is at college, he or she doesn't appear in the unemployment figures! The 2.3 million youngsters in higher education are responsible for over-optimistic annual employment figures, while allowing the government of the day to claim the credit for raising educational levels year on year.

When I finished my teaching career at a large High School in mid-Norfolk, it was the case that many of the students wanted to leave school and start work at the end of Y11: their ambitions lay in craft trades, agriculture, light engineering and – given the location of the school – the armed forces. Apart from those students in SEN groups, the majority were channelled away from these areas into college and university. (Of course, there was as ever a core of around 10% of very able, academically-gifted pupils who achieved excellent A/S grades and went on to study medicine, literature, science and other traditional courses.)

My personal belief is that this disgraceful manipulation of young people has resulted in generations of graduates saddled with massive debts and limited employment opportunities, while contributing to a worrying shortfall in trained crafts-men and women. This tends to explain why so many plumbers, nurses, agricultural workers and so on have to be recruited from overseas. If, after three years at college, you have a 2.1 in Film and TV studies, you're not going to want to try and pay off your student loan by working as a carrot picker on minimum wage.

A slightly more sinister thought: towards the end of my teaching career I became aware that the QCA syllabus being presented by high school science teachers (a percentage of whom had no scientific qualifications beyond GCE) included topics with heavily politicised content. For example, global warming was categorically stated to be anthropogenic, while alternative energy sources such as wind farms and solar power were endorsed with no opportunity for discussion of economic and environmental implications. Elsewhere in the school, other religions and moral codes, revisionist interpretations of history, alternative life styles and sexual orientation were not just discussed, they were actively promoted.

Universities and colleges have traditionally been centres of revolutionary thought, but this has not been the case in schools until comparatively recently. This, of course, allows education ministers of all political persuasions to build into the system the potential for ***indoctrination***, rather than ***education***.

In recent years there has been a significant attempt to recruit support from students, most overtly by the Labour Party. In the run-up to the 2017 General Election its then leader, Jeremy Corbyn, attended music festivals and concerts and went so far as to promise that a Labour government would give the vote to sixteen year olds! Call me an old cynic, but I'm not really keen on seeing major political decisions made at the polls by people who haven't even left school yet: what knowledge or understanding of the realities of life do children of sixteen bring to the ballot box?

Remember Naom Chomsky's identification of 'complacency in mediocrity' as an import-ant element in manipulation of the proletariat? I would argue that encouraging the belief that today's graduates with watered down degrees – often in basically recreational disciplines – are on a par with their peers elsewhere is an obvious example of this. You need only look at the UK's current ranking in international educational league tables (15th for Science, 27th for Maths, 22nd for Literacy) to see that the volume of graduates each year is not an indication of the ever-higher standards politicians would have you believe it is.

There is no disgrace in being of average intelligence and aptitude: by definition, the vast majority of us ***should be*** average! The problem arises when people are encouraged to believe that they are more able than they really are.

THE CONSPIRACY CONSPIRACY

This inevitably leads to unrealistic aspirations followed by resentment when these are unachievable.

Towards the end of my teaching career, I spent a few years working with some quite challenging pupils in an Educational Priority Area in eastern Norfolk. A disproportionate fraction of the boys (and a few girls) were 'on the books' of Premier League and Championship teams, often travelling miles after school and at the weekend for coaching courses at various 'soccer academies'. Every break time was spent kicking a football, while membership of a school team frequently resulted in time out of lessons. The sports staff encouraged the children in the belief that football could provide a fast track to wealth and fame: as a result many barely made any effort with their studies. To my certain knowledge, **not a single student** was ever given a contract as a professional player. The problem was, of course, that they had no plan B to fall back on. To a lesser extent many of the girls were similarly convinced they would one day be members of 'girl bands': at break and after school they rehearsed dance steps and vocal harmonies: again, with just a single exception (she became a dancer on a cruise liner), I don't recall any of them breaking into show business.

For some years the UK has been increasingly acknowledged as one of the global leaders in fine dining. Famous chefs from around the world have established restaurants in all major cities, while TV cookery programs and their celebrity hosts are followed by millions. I find it curious, therefore, that Home Economics (or Food Technology as it is increasingly labeled) is generally treated as a 'gap filler' in the school timetable. In many other western European countries, bar-tending, waiting, kitchen and front-of-house skills are seen as important opportunities for young people and can be studied to advanced levels, leading to higher paid, higher status careers in the service industries. This tends not to be the case in the UK, where, apart from the very top jobs, catering and hotel-related employment is thought of as menial. The single current exception to this is the phenomenon of the 'barista': this carefully chosen and promoted name for someone whose job fundamentally is to pour cups of milky coffee is yet another classic example of 'complacence in mediocrity': there is a lot more *cachet* in a job title that echoes a high position in the law, even if what you're actually doing is receiving around £8 an hour for a 35 hour week.

If nothing else, teaching school children about food might help them make better, more informed choices in life: a large proportion of young adults exist on a diet of takeaways and pre-prepared supermarket meals, which may be unhealthy, expensive or both!

Of course, there is nothing wrong in having aspirations: in my case I wanted to be an astronaut or a rock guitarist, which is why I joined the Navy as a pilot. When I realized that I was living in the wrong country to achieve the former and lacked the talent for the latter, I still had enough qualifications to allow a wide choice of alternative career. I would argue that ambition is a great motivator, as long as it is tempered by self-knowledge and realistic goals. If adults continually reinforce in children the idea that they can achieve absolutely **anything** regardless of their natural aptitude, the inevitable result is complacency in mediocrity.

Conspiracy theory

Education is routinely – and cynically – used by all parties as a political tool:

- Increasing the pass rate of public examinations by manipulation of grade curves misleads the public into believing that standards are improving.
- Keeping young people out of work longer removes over two million people from the 'job market' annually.
- Lack of high quality vocational training (and assigning lower status to trades and service industry jobs) denies employment opportunities to many school leavers and necessitates the use of migrant / immigrant workers
- The proliferation of non-academic University and CoFE courses encourages unrealistic ideas of personal achievement and, hence, promotes 'complacency in mediocrity'
- The lowering of educational standards and general

knowledge has resulted in an uncritical and credulous population that can be persuaded to believe almost anything they are told by 'experts': propaganda is readily mistaken for fact.

- The conclusions and opinions of genuinely independent researchers are easily marginalised or even dismissed, since fewer and fewer people are provided with the analytical skills to reach conclusions based on the logical consideration of all available data.

If all of this suggests some form of self-sustaining hereditary ruling elite (with occasional new recruits) here are some questions for which you might like to find answers

- Which schools and universities in the UK have generated the greatest number of religious, military, political and commercial leaders?

- Has **any** British political party ever put in place an educational system that genuinely gets the best out of **all** of the nation's population? Or is the highly confused modern teaching and examination provision actually intended to create the *illusion* of steady improvement in standards?

- Does government policy ultimately just provide the opportunity for a ruling elite to entrench its position?

- Does the modern **state** educational system generally encourage children to ask questions, think laterally and develop a thirst for knowledge? Or does it attempt to indoctrinate and institutionalize them and turn them into increasingly unquestioning 'citizen consumers'?

A final thought on this topic: on a recent edition of the quiz show 'Pointless', Richard Osman (the reputedly erudite question setter and checker) introduced a round on the subject of verbs by casually stating:

". . . because I went to a Comprehensive School in the 1980s, I have no idea what the definition of a verb is!"

THE CONSPIRACY CONSPIRACY

Chapter 3: Applied Science!

IT is a curious – and worrying – fact that the public's understanding of Science is diminishing at a time when its influence on their lives is daily increasing. As result, people have become ever more ready to accept the word of a 'scientific expert' even when it contradicts history and common sense.

Being well aware of this paradox, Politicians wishing to recruit public support for schemes that are potentially unpopular or of dubious value and/or legality will invariable involve scientific 'evidence' at some point.

Whether the UK government of the day is looking for an excuse to invade another sovereign state or kill off the badger population, there is always a scientist to justify the action. Additionally, tame scientific spokespersons are dragged in front of the media to deny the reality of phenomena of which millions of ordinary people have had personal experience.

Let's begin by examining how the role of politics in management of the countryside is often based on very dubious premises.

Unless you're a keen birdwatcher and you're over thirty years old, you've probably never heard of a Ruddy Duck.

THE CONSPIRACY CONSPIRACY

These engaging little waterfowl with their perky tails are resident in the United States, but began to breed in the UK in 1952 or thereabouts. It is probable that the original colonists were escapes from wildfowl collections such as Slimbridge in Gloucestershire, but it is not impossible that genuine American birds were involved too. Ducks are admirably suited to make the Atlantic crossing – if they get tired, they can drop on the water for a rest! In fact, thousands of American birds have made the crossing, including gulls, waders, egrets, cuckoos and even tiny warblers. Some have arrived in sufficient numbers to establish themselves as breeding species. Throughout the history of life on Earth, plants and animals have expanded their range and occupied new territories in just this way. Recent examples of additions to the British avifauna that have arrived from overseas include Little, Cattle and Great Egrets, Glossy Ibis, Spoonbill and Common Cranes. Other species that have flourished following intentional or accidental introductions include Pheasants, Red-legged Partridges, Little Owls, Ring-necked Parakeets, Red Kites and White-tailed Eagles.

The poor little Ruddy Duck, however, has two problems: it is notoriously randy and it has a distant relative in southern Europe: the White-headed Duck. Now this latter species is under enormous pressure from the draining of the Spanish and North African lakes it inhabits and – more significantly – from unregulated shooting. Any birdwatcher will tell you that the annual slaughter of migrating birds as they cross

THE CONSPIRACY CONSPIRACY

the Mediterranean region has resulted in dramatic declines in the populations of many once-familiar species: the Turtle Dove is a tragic recent example.

Back to the Ruddy Duck. For some reason British politicians and the conservation organization, the RSPB (doesn't the 'P' stand for 'protection'?) allowed themselves to be persuaded that occasional matings between 'our' Ruddy Ducks and their Spanish White-headed relatives was a greater threat than habitat loss and hunting! As a result the British Government sanctioned a cull of the Ruddy Duck that has seen a reduction in numbers from around 5500 to less than 100.

There are several flaws in the 'scientific justification' that the cull apologists trotted out for this action:

- The reported recovery of American Ruddy Ducks in the Azores suggests that they are capable of crossing the Atlantic under their own steam!
- Only a fraction of the Ruddy Ducks found elsewhere in Europe have been culled, leaving a reservoir to restock the UK and enjoy occasional holidays in Spain
- Wildlife conservation has observably been of very low priority in many Mediterranean countries: the decline of the White-headed Duck will probably continue due to numerous other factors.
- Why pick on the Ruddy Duck? Why not eliminate the Red-legged Partridge, the annual release of

THE CONSPIRACY CONSPIRACY

Plate 7: Ruddy Duck

which by game shoots has contributed towards the decimation of populations of our native Grey Partridge. Or how about the Grey Squirrel? The Chinese Water Deer? The Muntjac? Ring-necked Parakeet? All of these are implicated in the decline of native British species.

- Why take such draconian measures to protect an obscure and declining Spanish Duck while turning a blind eye to the annual slaughter of Mountain Hares, Hen Harriers and Buzzards by British gamekeepers and landowners?

THE CONSPIRACY CONSPIRACY

You'd have to believe that the Blair Government in 2003 (when the cull was initiated) was attempting to re-establish a level of international 'green' credibility following the possibly illegal and environmentally disastrous invasion of Iraq, while the RSPB is seen by many as an organisation that is continually trying to reinvent itself as a political force. This is, of course, far from being mandated by the majority of its members.

Both the Labour Government and the RSPB found no problem in locating 'conservationists' who were happy to endorse and justify the cull, possibly despite their personal views on the situation. There's a famous quote from the early days of spaceflight that is sort of relevant. When Gordon Cooper (one of the seven original American astronauts) was attempting to explain the importance of publicity in generating revenue for space exploration, he allegedly pointed to his Mercury-Redstone spacecraft and stated:

"Do you know what makes this bird fly? Funding! No bucks: no Buck Rogers!"

The same is absolutely the case in the scientific community: University faculties, research laboratories and government agencies all rely on continual streams of income to meet their high overheads. In return for funding, they are expected to come up with something new and worthwhile from time to time, despite what we are often led to believe about 'pure science'. Sometimes a suitable soundbite is enough to guarantee a few more months funding and not all

THE CONSPIRACY CONSPIRACY

scientists have shown themselves to be sufficiently altruistic to turn down the opportunity of an extended contract.

The same situation seems to apply with reference to the ongoing cull of Britain's largest carnivorous mammal, the Badger. Let's just think about the history of the man – cow – badger relationship:

Our ancestors occupy Britain, bringing their livestock with them. Their cattle are already infected with tuberculosis, which they then pass on to the resident Badger population. The Badgers infect or re-infect future generations of cattle, which complete the circle by infecting human beings. So we kill the Badgers. Doesn't seem very fair, does it?

Except it's not that simple a relationship: for a start, less than 1% of human TB cases develop from Bovine TB. To catch the disease you have to come into physical contact with faeces, urine, pus or exhaled air from an infected cow, or drink unpasteurised milk from one. None of these are likely to be a major possibility for city dwellers (or anyone apart from a farmer!) The vast majority of human TB is found among unimmunised immigrants from developing countries or elderly people whose historical infections sometimes flare up again in old age.

Another factor is that goats, pigs, cats and dogs can also carry the disease. Should we cull them too?

It needs to be born in mind that most of the milk we drink is pasteurised (for a variety of compelling reasons) and that immunisation against TB has been available for both

THE CONSPIRACY CONSPIRACY

livestock and humans for decades. However, the BCG test and immunisation many of us had in secondary school was discontinued in 2005, allegedly because the risk to modern children of catching TB was too low to warrant it. Instead 'targeted groups' received the vaccine, based on socio-economic background and geographical origin.

All this makes the case for eradicating our Badgers seem pretty thin, doesn't it? So what's the real agenda? It's pretty complex, but here is some data that is not disputed by either side of the argument:

- Badgers that are already infected with TB do not benefit from immunisation: uninfected Badgers do. There is a licensed, efficacious vaccine available that is currently in use in Wales.
- Testing all Badgers and culling **infected** individuals would be the most efficient option, but it is expensive: Badgers would have to be captured, tested and either immunised or destroyed humanely, involving large numbers of field-operatives for a long period.
- EU regulations do not allow the use of cattle vaccination as a method of controlling bTB.
- Cattle exports to the EU are worth over £300 million annually: trade with other nations adds about £100 million more.
- Revenue lost from the slaughter and disposal of cattle infected with bTB is around £100 million annually.

THE CONSPIRACY CONSPIRACY

- The first two years of the Badger cull cost British taxpayers around £6,500 **per Badger**.

The whole situation is extremely complex and has generated emotional response in people that are neither involved in farming nor wildlife conservation. Both sides of the debate are presented on television by celebrities and politicians, usually supported by scientific experts: we are invited to choose who we believe, based upon the evidence. However, because of the marginalisation of Science in schools, a large proportion of the population are not equipped to make a logical decision: their response (either way) is almost entirely emotional. Ultimately the cull will continue because:

- The Government, rather than aging pop stars, has the final say.
- The farming lobby is very powerful and generally gets its own way because of the high-value export trade in meat, livestock and cereals.
- It is easier for the Government to recruit scientists to support the cull, because it generally pays their wages or provides funding for their research.

I shall return to environmental issues in the next chapter, but for now let's move on to how some other areas of Science have been hijacked by orthodoxy for political ends.

Given the provision of free education to the age of 18 in most countries on the planet, you wouldn't think it possible that there is a growing number of people who believe that

THE CONSPIRACY CONSPIRACY

the Earth is flat – but, even in the US and the UK, that is the case. You can present as much anecdotal evidence as you like, but 'flat earthers' have their own observations to counter it:

- The curvature of the Earth can be seen during high altitude flight or from space.
- *You can't see the alleged curvature from a commercial airliner or the top of a mountain: no-one has actually travelled in space.*
- If you stand on the seashore and watch a boat sailing towards the horizon, it can be seen to diminish as it moves over the distant curve of the Earth, until all you see are its upperworks and masts.
- *This is an optical illusion based on aerial perspective and the structure of the human eye.*
- The Earth's circular shadow can be seen crossing the Moon during a lunar eclipse.
- *The shadow merely proves that the Earth is circular, not spherical.*

Because the general level of scientific knowledge in the western world is observably in decline, the extraordinary ideas above are increasingly gaining support. Predictably, the establishment has frequently seized the opportunity for a response of the 'scatter gun' variety, lumping the ludicrous flat Earth belief in with a number of unrelated phenomena that are embarrassing or unacceptable to conventional science, even though **all** of these are based on far more evidence and much sounder logic.

(Ironically, theoretical cosmologists are increasingly debating models of the universe that make a belief in UFOs and EBEs seem very tame: a current example is that our universe is a three dimensional projection of a two dimensional hologram!)

Some examples of widely held beliefs based upon innumerable personal experiences that are dismissed by scientific orthodoxy include:

- The reality of a significant percentage of reports of anomalous aerial phenomena (OK: UFOs!).
- The existence of large, unknown anthropoids in several regions of the world (Bigfoot, Yeti, Almas etc.).
- The existence of ghosts and similar apparitions.
- The crop circle phenomenon: not all structures are provably man-made.
- The existence of large, unknown aquatic animals (Sea Serpents, Megalodon, lake monsters etc.).
- Anomalous technology: archaeological discoveries of anachronistic devices.

There's probably been more than enough written on some of these topics, but I just want to add a few personal anecdotes and thoughts on a couple of these, in order to illustrate how they have been unjustifiably marginalised –

ridiculed, even – by the establishment. At the same time, it's worth taking the time to reflect on possible motives behind this.

The UFO phenomenon

I first became interested in 'flying saucers' and other anomalous aerial phenomena as early as 1957, for the excellent reason that I had my first personal experience (a silver daylight disc) as a six year-old boy in the early months of that year.

This sighting began a lifetime's interest and research and now, in my sixties, I have met and spoken with dozens of Astronauts (including at least one 'Moonwalker' from each of the six alleged lunar landings) scores of famous aviators and hundreds of very credible witnesses. These include famous astronomers, politicians, high-ranking military personnel and ordinary people who have had extraordinary experiences.

Since my first 'close encounter of the first kind', I have witnessed perhaps a further half a dozen objects that (even as a professional astronomer and ex-pilot) I cannot explain. For many years I was careful not to mention my experiences and beliefs in my private or professional life, but a chance meeting in a Norfolk bar caused me to rethink.

In the early nineteen eighties (while still working as a full-time teacher!) I spent my evenings running a hotel bar in the Norfolk Broads region. The location of the Hotel (near two major RAF bases) meant that service men and women from both the RAF and USAF regularly dropped in. One of these (whose identity I can't reveal here) was a serving Radar Operator/Fighter Controller at an important base in the heart of Broadland. His role was to monitor uncorrelated incursions into UK airspace: usually these could quickly be identified as Soviet 'Bear' bombers, probing the UK's state of readiness. Sometimes they would be American aircraft making emergency approaches to the nearby fighter station – I myself witnessed SR71 'Blackbird' and U2 spy planes doing just that.

The RAF Sergeant and I shared an interest in space exploration and aviation which, on one memorable occasion, prompted him to discuss the strange events he had been witness to over the Christmas period in 1980.

His then wife being based overseas on Ascension Island, my friend had readily agreed to take the unpopular Christmas watch-keeping duty. Christmas Day was quiet, as was most of the evening. However, things became more interesting in the early hours of Boxing Day, when an uncorrelated return appeared on his radar screen. The station's Type 84 radar (with its range of over 400km) had detected a solid object apparently entering UK airspace over the North Sea before ultimately crossing the Suffolk Coast near Woodbridge. My informant discovered that this incursion had been detected by other radar bases in the **Improved United Kingdom Air Defence Ground Environment** and had been recorded by the Master Control Centre at West Drayton.

Plate 8: Author with Charles Halt

I found my friend's account intriguing to say the least and have spent the intervening 38 years investigating what was to evolve into the 'Rendlesham Forest UFO Incident'. Full accounts of this are available online and in a number of well-researched books (and a few that are downright fantasy!)

I have been fortunate enough to have met – and lectured alongside – the Deputy Base Commander of RAF Bentwaters at the time, Col. Charles Halt, USAF. This highly credible and plain-speaking officer has had to endure ridicule and even unbelievable levels of hostility since he decided to reveal his role in the incident. To me, however, his account supports much of the testimony of the two other USAF personnel to have come forward with their accounts, Sgt James Penniston and A1C John Burrows. Having listened at first hand to their versions of events, I'm certain that something extremely strange took place over a couple of nights and that the conventional explanations involving lightships, lighthouses, re-entry of Soviet satellites and exploding fireballs are glib and insulting to the main participants, who have stuck to their basic stories for nearly forty years. (See bibliography for some suggested further reading).

As a professional meteoriticist, I have been somewhat disappointed by the manner in which several people in the field of Astronomy have rushed to dismiss the Woodbridge Incident in the most trivial of terms: often their 'explanations' bear no relationship to the actual events, but are accepted as such by the media. One populist author has continually championed the explanation that a group of experienced military personnel spent two nights chasing the beam of a distant lighthouse around Rendlesham Forest, despite the fact that, following extended service in the area, all were completely familiar with its appearance.

If your only data input is the TV, the tabloids or online news roundups such as MSN, you might imagine that such events are very infrequent. In fact, nothing could be further

THE CONSPIRACY CONSPIRACY

from the truth: as you read this, someone, somewhere in the UK is looking at an unfamiliar object or light in the sky. The majority of these will be explainable in terms of conventional aircraft, meteorological or astronomical phenomena or birds. Some will be fabrications or hoaxes. But some – more than you'd imagine – are truly inexplicable. Author and ex-Police Officer John Hanson has spent years compiling his **magnum opus**, the 'Haunted Skies' series. Currently numbering over a dozen volumes, these painstakingly-researched books contain hundreds of thousands of credible accounts by a complete spread of professions and backgrounds within the UK, from farmers and road-menders to pilots, police officers and peers of the realm.

So why is Hanson's material not better-known? Why is he never consulted by the producers of TV and radio programmes, rather than media light-weights with little or no background knowledge of the UFO phenomenon? Why is particle physicist and media-darling Brian Cox allowed to assert unchallenged on the Rob Brydon Show in 2012 that:

"No UFOs have ever landed, no-one's been abducted – it's all bollocks!"

Prof. Cox is, of course, entitled to his opinion, just as I'm entitled to mine about his contribution to popular culture as a member of ephemeral music group 'D-Ream'. (The Prof. is no Brian May!). But the outpourings of people like Cox should not be confused with fact: he has no basis for making such dismissive statements about an area which he has never studied, any more than I have in holding forth about particle physics.

Many UFO researchers see something more sinister than just scepticism in Prof. Cox's comments. He so frequently and freely comes out with his uninformed and negative soundbites that some suspect he is part of an orchestrated strategy to convince the public that the whole 'UFO thing' has no basis in fact. What is indicative of Cox's role as 'pet boffin' is that he is increasingly chosen to present documentaries on subjects about which he has absolutely no background knowledge. Astronomy, evolution, zoology, geology: there is nothing about which he isn't prepared to give an opinion! He is the default go-to Scientist, even though many less well-known but better-qualified among his peers cringe at some of his pronouncements. Need a quote to trivialise the UFO phenomenon? Alien Abduction? The Moon Landing Conspiracy? Phone up Prof. Brian! He once posted this response on Twitter:

"I've said it before and I'll say it again: if you don't think Apollo 11 landed on [the] Moon, you are a colossal nob end and should get a new brain"

You might wish that you'd been educated to PhD level so you could make such informed and well-crafted arguments! (Mind you, he seems to have missed the lectures on spelling and composition!)

In some ways this has echoes of the way in which the late and rightly lamented Sir Patrick Moore publicly ridiculed a belief in the idea of extraterrestrial visitors to our part of the Solar System, despite having claimed to have found an artificial structure on the Moon and having described how he met a 'Man from Mars' in a book he published under a pseudonym.

But is there a policy of disinformation and obfuscation about the UFO phenomenon? And if so, why should this be?

It seems to me there are a number of reasons why governments around the world might attempt to mislead their populations or suppress evidence about UFOs: some, perhaps, with less obvious and more sinister motives than others:

- Governments are worried that definite proof of the existence of extraterrestrials and their palpably superior technology might cause widespread fear and panic.

- The belief in other, totally unrelated forms of intelligent life in the Universe is contrary to the creation beliefs of most of the world's religions. Any government presenting proof of this would inevitably incur the anger – or worse – of fundamentalists of all faiths.

- Several governments (or clandestine groups outside the establishment) are actively collaborating with extraterrestrials in order to benefit from exclusive use of some of their superior technology.

THE CONSPIRACY CONSPIRACY

- Senior world leaders are aware of a real and present threat to our continued existence from hostile EBEs (extraterrestrial biological entities), but see no point in broadcasting the fact until negotiations are concluded – or suitable technological responses are in place!

If all this seems a little far-fetched, it may be worth reflecting on how the media (particularly TV and film companies) manipulate our image and opinions of EBEs. For a long time extraterrestrials were portrayed as generally friendly: sometimes even as ancient, wise and keen to help the human race progress **('Close Encounters', 'Batteries Not Included', 'ET', 'The Day The Earth Stood Still', 'Paul').**

On other occasions they are presented as hostile, coldly calculating and indifferent to our fate **('War Of The Worlds', 'Independence Day', 'Mars Attacks', 'Battle Of Los Angeles').**

Recently, some very powerful and influential politicians, industrialists and military personnel have seemingly endorsed the second of these versions. It will be interesting to see how things progress!

Inconvenient anthropology

If we are to believe orthodox palaeontology, all humans on the planet are descended from ancestral forms that evolved in the Rift Valley of East Africa around five to seven million years ago. From this region, we are told, our ancestors spread across the planet evolving into increasingly large and sophisticated forms of several species, ultimately culminating in the first true humans.

The oldest fossil remains of Homo sapiens were discovered at Jebel Irhoud, Morocco in 1961, but not recognised as such until far more recently. Unfortunately for supporters of the accepted East African genesis, these have been dated at around 300,000 years, far older than the 195,000 and 160,000-year-old remains from Omo Kibish and Herto, in Ethiopia. Further inconvenience has been caused to pragmatic anthropology by the discovery in Bulgaria and Greece of fossils that seem to be of the oldest pre-humans yet discovered. At 7.2 million years old, Graecopithecus freybergi is widely recognized as representing the first divergence from the last common ancestor of humans and chimpanzees. Increasingly, therefore, it would appear that the 'cradle of mankind' might possibly have been the Balkans rather than East Africa.

The Book of the Damned, published in 1919, was the first book written by American journalist Charles Fort, arguably the greatest ever recorder of inconvenient and anomalous phenomena. The 'damned' in the title are items or pieces of data that so challenge orthodoxy that they are simply ignored or buried in museums and archives. (Some interesting examples will be discussed later!)

The discovery that the oldest pre-human remains on the planet are those of Graecopithecus is a strong contender for

THE CONSPIRACY CONSPIRACY

Fortean damnation, because it doesn't fit with the official line that there has only been one human genesis. Why should this be a problem? The answer has nothing to do with science and everything to do with politics and religion.

Virtually all of the world's religions begin with a creation myth of some sort: this generally involves a deity creating the Earth and its animals and plants, followed by the first man and woman from whom the rest of humanity is descended. (As a six year-old I was 'encouraged' to attend Sunday school: after a couple of weeks I was banned for asking the obvious question: 'If God created Adam and Eve and they only had two **sons**, where did **we** come from?')

Since being adopted and reinvented by the Romans in the fourth century, Christianity has undergone numerous dogmatic and political mutations. In its modern incarnation, it promotes itself as a religion of universal brotherhood, fraternity, peace and forgiveness. (Adherents of the various Christian Churches tend not to reminisce about the 'good old days' of crusading, anti-Jewish pogroms, inquisitions and wholesale destruction of native American and Latin-American civilizations.)

The Anglican Church's big reinvention began with the antislavery movement of the nineteenth century, followed eventually by the dismantling of the British Empire and full emancipation of its subjects. Against this background, Charles Darwin published 'On the Origin of Species' and the first palaeontologists (Lyell, Mantell, Owen and others) began to demonstrate that life on Earth has been the product of many gradual changes over millions of years.

The establishment naturally found this extremely challenging, since it appeared to disprove the biblical genesis story: this, it was feared, might easily lead to the Church being replaced by humanism and atheism. Bear in mind that at that time the power of both the Monarchy and Parliament were inextricably linked to the Church of England and you can easily see why religious leaders and politicians needed to regroup!

In the Genesis creation story in the Old Testament, humans are stated to have been created by God in his own image: but this was – and continues to be – at odds with the observable fact that mankind occurs in a wide range of colours, shapes and sizes. Central to the Theory of Evolution is the assumption that all of these evolved from a common ape-like ancestor. The Church and establishment had therefore to look for a way to restore the Biblical 'specialness' of human

Plate 9: Two different subspecies of Wagtails – virtually indistinguishable

beings: this was achieved by assigning them all to a single species: Homo sapiens.

If anyone then or **now** were to question this, they would certainly be labelled a racist or supremacist, yet the physical differences between the **races** of mankind are often far more obvious than the subtle distinctions between many **species** of animal or plant.

That the majority of these differences in physical appearance are the result of long evolutionary processes in response to environmental factors is not disputed: examples would be the eyelid fold and sparse facial hair of the oriental races (generally conceded to have evolved as protections against snow-glare and frostbite from frozen beards) and the fair skin, hair and lack of iris pigmentation of the northern European races (white surfaces are very poor radiators of heat energy: hence the typical Scandinavian coloration significantly reduces body heat loss).

These genotypic/phenotypic differences and the possibility that the Moroccan and Balkan ancestral remains may indicate more than one prehistoric origin for mankind also inevitably suggests that modern man represents more than a single species. The fact that these can successfully produce perfectly healthy offspring together does not preclude this: as we have seen, the same is true of the White-headed Duck and Ruddy Duck, which are two separate species native to different continents. Even more relevant is the fact that it is now generally accepted that Homo sapiens and

Homo neanderthalensis freely interbred, so much so that the chromosomes of modern man carry genes from both.

The existence of other hominids clinging on to survival in remote regions of the planet would also necessitate a rethink of the genetic origins of mankind: this is perhaps one of the reasons why orthodoxy dismisses the possibility out of hand.

Large legendary hominids such as the Yeti, Almas, Sasquatch and Swamp Ape may or may not represent prehistoric survivals into modern times, but the fact that stories of very similar semi-mythical ape-men are found in the folk tales of Europe, Asia, and North America are at least suggestive that they may have done so until comparatively recently.

Despite compelling video and photographs, hair and tissue samples and literally thousands of eye-witness accounts, scientific orthodoxy continues to deny even the possibility that these might be evidence of actual flesh and blood hominids, let alone allocate any serious effort or resources on a search for them. The reason generally given on the occasional light-hearted TV documentary is that scientists have more pressing demands on their time and resources, but the truth may not be as simple as that. A ***successful*** quest that conclusively proved the existence of the very man-like North American Bigfoot, for example, would tend to indicate a completely new and separate branch of human evolution. (It's worth recalling that apes are currently unknown from both North and South America).

Anomalous Technology

Charles Fort's exhaustive researches are commemorated in the adjective **fortean**, which is applied to phenomena which seem to challenge generally-held beliefs and apparently defy conventional science. The majority can usually be explained satisfactorily, but there are still a number that cannot.

The nineteen sixties and seventies numerous saw the release of innumerable works that attempted to prove that some of mankind's greatest megalithic structures were either built by our ancestors with the assistance of alien benefactors, or were their attempts to replicate poorly-understood alien technology. Many of these books made their authors rich and famous, despite some glaring errors and fabrications. Even now there are a number of cable TV networks airing series based around the 'Ancient Astronaut' genre: many of these make the most outrageous claims and assumptions based on pseudo-scientific mumbo-jumbo. Typical of this was a recent documentary that sought to claim that a group of vaguely pyramid-shaped hills in Bosnia are not only artificial, but were built to transmit 'standing waves' to the cosmos at faster-than-light speed. Hmmm….

As is often the case, archaeological orthodoxy has seized the opportunity to group ludicrous claims such as this alongside other, less-easily dismissed discoveries.

There **are** several astonishingly modern-looking artefacts that are indisputably ancient. There are also plenty of objects that have turned up in 'impossible' locations. These include:

- The Antikythera Mechanism (a complex structure of toothed wheels and levers that is acknowledged to be some form of astronomical calculator)

- The Baghdad Battery: if this object is not a simple device for generating low-voltage electrical power, it's hard to imagine what it might be! A recent recreation of the device produced an output of 4 volts.

- The Calixtlahuaca Head: a terracotta bust found in a late 15th century Mexican tomb is widely considered to be a second century Roman sculpture, begging the question of how it crossed the Atlantic 1200 years before Columbus!

There are several ways of explaining anomalous discoveries such as these: we could, for example, be placing modern interpretations of design and function on ancient items whose purpose we don't fully understand. Objects such as the Calixtlahuaca Head could have arrived in Mexico in a variety of other ways than aboard a Roman Galley. They could have been made – or planted – more recently than suggested.

There are, however some structures that seem to defy all the received wisdom about our ancestors' levels of knowledge and technological skill. Unconventional theories proposed by researchers thinking more laterally about their construction are among the 'damned' that tend to be ridiculed out of hand.

THE CONSPIRACY CONSPIRACY

Some amazing examples that are incapable of explanation in conventional terms include:

- **The Sacsayhuaman Walls**

    These massive fortifications in Peru are generally credited to the Inca, who are believed to have constructed them in the thirteenth century. The three concentric walls, measuring 360 metres in length and 6 metres in height, are built without mortar from huge blocks weighing up to 300 tons. It genuinely is the case that the enormous irregular polygonal stones are so accurately carved and assembled that a fine knife blade cannot be inserted between them. Yet we are told that the stones were quarried and finished using river pebbles! There is no Inca tradition about how the stones were dressed so accurately, although a legend collected by explorer Percy Fawcett claimed that the builders used a plant extract to soften the stone!

- **Baalbek**

    This important Roman temple complex in Lebanon is built upon a more ancient platform constructed from enormous dressed limestone blocks: the western retaining wall includes the 'Three Stones', each weighing around 800 tons. At a nearby quarry can be seen two unused stones with estimated weights of 1000 and 1200 tons. Conventional explanations

Plate 10: Baalbek

of how, when and why these were quarried, dressed and moved invariably involve hundreds of thousands of man-hours and stone tools.

- **Nan Madol**

    Built between 1180 and 1200 AD on a coral reef on the edge of the Pacific island of Pohnpei in Micronesia, this ancient complex of over one hundred artificial islands connected by canals and causeways is constructed from ***a quarter of a billion tons*** of basalt. Even local legends are ambiguous about who built the structures, how they did it and exactly why.

THE CONSPIRACY CONSPIRACY

Conspiracy theory

Scientific validation is increasingly used to support dubious practices and ridicule innovative thought that challenges orthodoxy.

- Since academic researchers often have to compete for public funding, they are open to recruitment by interest groups to supply a rationale for potentially unpopular actions or policies based on dubious or disputed scientific premises.

- Levels of knowledge are so basic in many areas that assertions by experts are rarely challenged. Children in British primary schools are still taught that the Egyptian pyramids were built by slaves using rollers to move the large stones into place, despite the fact that the Egyptians did not have a slavery culture and, arguably, did not have access to sufficient trees to make the necessary rollers.

- Inconvenient discoveries in the fields of archaeology and palaeontology that suggest alternative and radical datings for key events in the development of life on Earth are generally ignored, hidden or ridiculed, especially if they apparently contradict religious, ethical or political dogma.

Chapter 4: The Conservation Game

FOR a number of years I have maintained a daily natural history blog to record the wildlife of East Norfolk. This has built up a decent following and generated some animated discussion both online and in the field. Unlike many others, the blog is not primarily intended to be political, nor does it attempt to sway public opinion: it's just a photo diary of my wildlife observations, with occasional bits of astronomy that I've found interesting. Apart from occasional forays into Suffolk, most of my expeditions are within a few miles of my front door.

Naturally, I keep an eye on other people's blogs, as well as a number of the many Twitter feeds from my part of the country – this is often my first source of information about rare or unusual species that turn up during periods of migration. The title of this section is taken from the biographical details on the blog of a Norfolk reserve manager:

"I'm in my early 30's and have been in the conservation game for the past 8 years"

Conservation **game**? To me, this quote seems to provide an insight into the thinking of many involved in the modern environmental movement: I can't imagine Sir Peter Scott or Ted Ellis choosing the phrase to describe their work.

Soon after I started monitoring these 'blogs and tweets', I became aware of a fascinating double standard among some of the people who write them. A fair number of these are employed as ecologists or staff (paid or voluntary) on wildlife reserves: others are Environmental Science undergraduate or postgraduate students. Their published thoughts almost invariably contain a large element of opinion and theory about reasons for the decline in wildlife populations and the role of technology in climate change and habitat loss. Without exception among the online publications I follow, human carbon dioxide emissions are given as the ***indisputable*** cause of global warming. I'll return to that sacred cow in a page or two!

The double standard I referred to earlier is the fact that many of these earnest young eco-warriors seem to spend a considerable part of their time travelling the globe 'monitoring changing wildlife populations', (while coincidentally adding to their world life-lists!) Recently I came across several accounts of groups and individuals carrying out seabird surveys on remote Pacific islands as part of their PhD studies: nice work if you can get it!

Additionally, a surprisingly large number of these environmental activists (as they often style themselves) earn a full or part-time living as guides on organised bird tours. Recent

THE CONSPIRACY CONSPIRACY

destinations I've noted have included Costa Rica, Ethiopia, Cuba and Kazakhstan. Bear in mind, the guide's role on these excursions is to guarantee that the participants (who have often paid very large sums to take part) see as many as the endemic birds as possible: this, naturally, involves plenty of driving too. Here's an intriguing and undisputed fact: **each passenger's share** of the CO_2 emitted by a Boeing 747 in flying to Florida is about the same as that produced by a typical British family car **in a year!**

Birdwatching as a pleasant rural pastime for gentlemen has been around for over a century, but its popularity exploded in the nineteen eighties. It replaced angling as the outdoor pursuit *du jour* and expensive binoculars, spotting 'scopes and camera equipment became the tools of the trade of the 'serious' birder.

Within birdwatching is a 'hardcore' element, usually referred to as **twitching**. This is the single-minded pursuit of rare birds, often in order to add them to various personal 'seen' lists. These might include local patch lists, year lists, UK lists, Western Palaearctic lists and world lists. Rivalry between serious **listers** can be extreme, often escalating into online insults and disputes and even, occasionally, actual violence! The current UK Champion lister (from Norfolk!) has a British list of 600 species, while, at the time of writing, the greatest World List amassed (by a retired British naval officer) is an incredible 9,047 species of a possible ten and a half thousand. (I'm a bit of a casual twitcher myself: despite being a retired naval officer living in Norfolk, however, my British list is a paltry 430 or so!)

A brief search through Twitter will reveal frequent accounts of long distance 'twitches' both in the UK and in mainland Europe. (Recent records of Blue Rock Thrush, Amur Falcon and Siberian Rubythroat saw many of the twitching fraternity setting off on long car, boat and air journeys to the extremities of the British Isles. I have, however, yet to hear a young birder/twitcher acknowledge that his hobby is dramatically increasing his annual carbon footprint...)

I'm certain that most of the young birders involved genuinely don't see their actions as conflicting with their political and environmental beliefs: I'm sure many of them feel that the knowledge acquired spending a month as a volunteer on Fair Isle or leading a tour group to Nepal will contribute towards saving the planet. The only problem I have with this philosophy is the frequency with which I am told that my generation is responsible for the destruction of the natural environment. Let's examine that claim!

For fifteen years I was Head of Environmental, Rural and Agricultural Sciences at a large Norfolk High School: as I mentioned earlier, I was part of a panel that set syllabuses and wrote examinations for these subjects. As long ago as 1976 The Greenhouse Effect was a required element of CSE studies, as were units on pollution, over-use of agrochemicals, conservation and eco-friendly approaches in agriculture. At the time the contribution made to climate change by 'greenhouse gases' such as carbon dioxide (CO_2) and methane (CH_4) was just beginning to be discussed. Instead of the near-hysterical apocalyptic predictions and blame-apportioning we see now, the debate was more considered and rational: both sides of the argument were encouraged to present the evidence they had gathered and the conclusions they had reached from processing it. Then politicians and businessmen became involved and everything changed...

The global climate is changing: there can be no disputing that fact. The atmosphere and oceans are gradually warming with inevitable changes to ocean currents and winds. But the climate is ***always*** changing: there have been very few stable periods in the Earth's four and a half billion year history. There have been long spells when ice sheets have spread over large areas of both hemispheres and others when the continents were covered by hot, arid deserts. At the moment the planet is still recovering from the most recent Ice Age: there is a long way to go to return to the ambient temperatures of the last interglacial period that ended 115,000 years ago. At that time temperatures in the Arctic were 8°C higher and sea levels up to 12 metres higher than today and the British fauna included rhinoceros, straight-tusked elephants and hippopotamus.

Despite what we are frequently invited to believe, the natural mechanisms that trigger an ice age (or conclude one) are poorly understood. This has allowed anthropogenic climate change enthusiasts to hijack the data and somehow use it to support their position. What is never discussed these days is the possibility that fluctuations in radiation arriving from space make a significant contribution to changes in the Earth's 'heat budget'.

How many of you are aware that the polar gaps of Mars also show rhythmic cycles of growth and shrinking? According to Michael Malin, NASA chief scientist on the Mars Orbiter Camera, the northern polar ice cap is disappearing at:

". . . a prodigious rate. The images, documenting changes from 1999 to 2005, suggest the climate on Mars is presently warmer, and perhaps getting warmer still, than it was several decades or centuries ago."

A number of planetary scientists are convinced that the Martian warming is largely due to increasing solar output, which might also explain some of the recent warming of the Earth. Another external factor is the up and down oscillation of the Sun and solar system through the plane of our galaxy, The Milky Way.

I'd put money on it that most of those reading this will have never read anywhere else about this. It's another example of 'damned' fortean data! The period of this oscillation is around seventy million years, so that every thirty five million years the Solar System passes through the galactic midplane. As it does so, the amount of cosmic radiation that arrives on the Earth increases dramatically for a period of around one hundred thousand years. You might imagine that sub-atomic particles and radiation from distant stars would contribute little or nothing to atmospheric energy, but in fact the amount that arrives in this way every second over each 3km x 3km region of the Earth would power a 60 watt light bulb. That is a vast amount of energy over the whole surface of the globe: over three billion watts a second, which, as we have noted above, increases many times every thirty five million years. As far as I know, this contribution to atmospheric warming and its rhythmic nature has never been widely acknowledged as a factor in climate change.

As I stated above, there can be little doubt that the Earth's atmosphere is currently warming: the contentious issues are why, what will be the impact on us and is there anything we can do about it.

You'll recall the principle of government that I identified in the introduction:

PROBLEM – REACTION – SOLUTION

This is particularly relevant to a discussion of climate change. Obscure research into habitat change and loss back in the nineteen sixties led to academic conjecture about its causes and implications to mankind. It's often forgotten these days that the initial prediction was that the planet was close to reaching a climate 'tipping point' that would trigger a new ice age. (There were even a few big budget Hollywood films released based on this scenario.)

Politicians and industrialists quickly saw the opportunity to hijack the idea of anthropogenic global warming and began to use it to further their own policies:

THE CONSPIRACY CONSPIRACY

- **PROBLEM**: Mankind's ever-increasing release of greenhouse gases is increasing the temperature of the oceans and atmosphere, leading inevitably to melting of the polar caps, raising of sea levels, widespread flooding, dramatic reductions in food production and the destruction of the world's natural ecosystems.

- **REACTION**: A public clamour for something to be done, apportioning of blame, attacks on anyone with a contradictory opinion of the situation.

- **SOLUTION**: Legislation ostensibly aimed at reducing CO_2 emissions through increased fuel and travel taxation. Rapid expansion of industries involved in the development of alternative 'renewable' energy sources and technologies.

I occasionally wonder if the earlier drama associated with the destruction of the ozone layer was a 'dry run' for the global warming main event.

In 1985 Joseph Farman, Brian Gardiner, and Jonathan Shanklin (researchers from the Polar Institute in Cambridge) published a paper announcing a rhythmic fluctuation in the density of the ozone layer over the Antarctic. Ozone is a triatomic oxygen molecule that is continually generated from oxygen as solar and cosmic radiation strikes the upper layers of the atmosphere. A **very** simplified equation of this reaction would be:

$$O_2 + O \rightleftharpoons O_3$$

The ozone molecules thus formed are unstable and continually break apart and reform. The importance of this to us is that in this way the energy used to form the bond is absorbed rather than reaching the Earth's surface: UV and other radiations are known to be a cause of skin cancers.

A couple of years after the announcement of polar ozone depletion, other researchers identified a possible cause: the CFC (chlorofluorocarbon) gas extensively used at the time as the propellant in aerosols and coolant in refrigerators. Even now I'm surprised that no-one queried this immediately. The two ozone holes are above the poles: I'm not aware that Polar Bears and Penguins are heavy users of deodorants, nor that Inuit houses contain significantly more fridges and air conditioners than those in the rest of the world!

Of course, the discovery of the hole in the ozone layer was immediately used to justify a widespread ban on the use of CFCs and redesign of devices that used it. I have to say: I'm not a huge fan of spray cans – cream tastes a lot better from a jug – and atomisers have been used for perfume for a century. The search for an alternative coolant for refrigerators and air conditioners took a little more thought.

It's a curious and ironic fact that Thomas Midgley, the chemist largely responsible for CFCs, also discovered the 'anti-knock' properties of lead tetraethyl when added to petrol. The poor man died in 1944 thinking he would be remembered as a hero of the modern age but is regarded by eco-warriors in exactly opposite terms!

THE CONSPIRACY CONSPIRACY

The virtual CFC monopoly initially enjoyed by American company DuPont and its product **Freon** was gradually eroded by other chemical producers, so that the US and European ban on the substance had greater potential impact on China and India, the world's leading producers at the time. CFCs were briefly replaced by HFCs, but when these were identified as greenhouse gases a reduction in *their* production was called for (and agreed to by signatories of the Kigali Agreement).

Guess who are the leading manufacturers of the only current environmentally-friendly alternative? Correct! Two US companies!

As seems to be taken for granted these days, the world's 'rich countries' are expected to stump up a considerable sum ($540 million) to compensate 'poor' countries like India (!) for lost revenue from HFC production. See what I mean about the CFC crisis looking like a dry run of the global warming saga? A cynic might suggest that the industrial-political complex, having proved to their satisfaction that environmental alarms are a very useful tool in manipulating public opinion, moved on to phase two.

If you enjoy reading detective novels, you'll have come across the main investigative technique (of fictional detectives at least!) When a crime has been committed, ask yourself who had the best

THE CONSPIRACY CONSPIRACY

- **Means**
- **Motive**
- **Opportunity**

What holds true for Mr Holmes and M. Poirot also holds true in the world of conspiracy! To identify the perpetrators of what may be one of the biggest cons in history, we need to apply these principles to anthropogenic global warming.

I don't want to bore you with pages of statistics, entrenched opinion and political posturing. Let's just simplify things into a bulleted summary:

- There has been a gradual rise in ocean and atmospheric temperatures: this has been interpreted by many scientists and climatologists (but far from all) as being the result of increased atmospheric concentrations, in particular, of carbon dioxide from car exhausts, power stations and industrial plants. The climate changes claimed to be produced by these emissions have been collated and presented graphically: these graphs seem to predict a hysteresis rise in global temperatures with dramatic implications for the human race.

Look closely at the following graph: notice that the vertical axis only allows data to be plotted in a very narrow range (56°F – 59°F). Compare this to the graph below it, where the vertical axis covers a much more realistic range of global temperatures: the horizontal axis has the same scale on both graphs.

THE CONSPIRACY CONSPIRACY

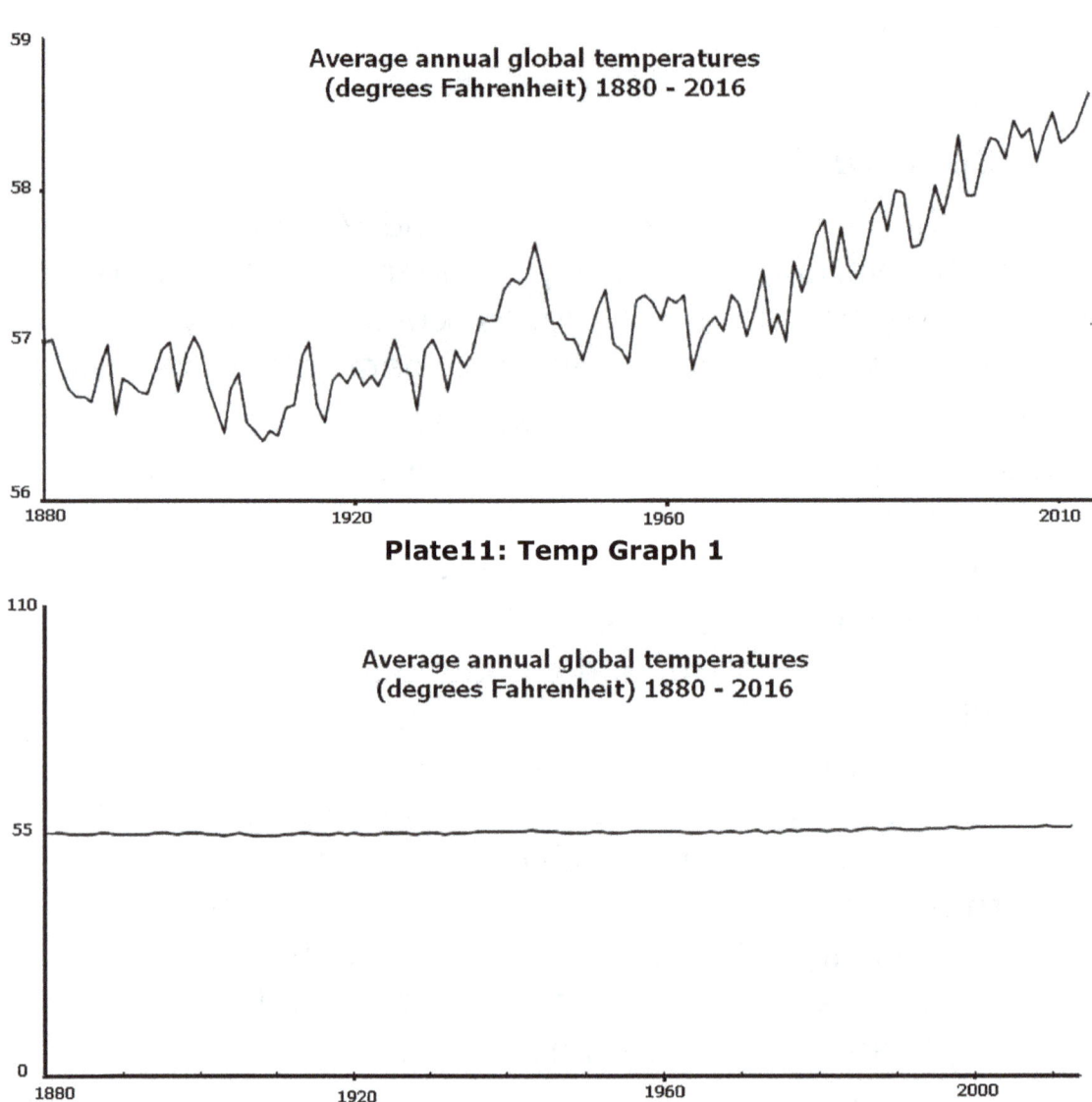

Plate11: Temp Graph 1

Plate12: Temp Graph 2

These graphs use exactly the same sets of data, but the axes have been carefully chosen to support the two diametrically opposed points of view. Furthermore, no modern scientist uses the Fahrenheit scale, but it has been

THE CONSPIRACY CONSPIRACY

chosen over the centigrade scale because it generates a greater vertical distortion of the data. In reality, both graphs reveal a temperature increase of around 1°F in 130 years...

- Human production of greenhouse gases (particularly carbon dioxide and sulphur dioxide) has increased steadily since the start of the Industrial Revolution and as a result of the greenhouse effect is beyond question the major factor in global warming. The invention of the internal combustion engine has accelerated the rate at which atmospheric changes are taking place. Only drastic reductions in greenhouse gas emissions can bring a halt to runaway global warming and prevent an unimaginable catastrophe.

This statement is the central argument in support of anthropogenic global warming. Taken at face value it seems a powerful piece of evidence that human activities are the cause of increasing concentrations of atmospheric CO_2. But does it truly reflect the facts? Are the levels now really the highest they have ever been? And are there no other sources of carbon dioxide?

The answer to both questions is linked to molluscs! This ancient and highly successful invertebrate phylum includes gastropods (slugs and snails) bivalves (clams, mussels, oysters, etc.) and cephalopods (squids and octopuses) as well as a few other living and extinct classes.

Although most of these are still frequently encountered, they were once even more abundant: so much so that whole mountain ranges are made from their shells.

THE CONSPIRACY CONSPIRACY

The shells of bivalves and some cephalopods are made of calcium carbonate: since the appearance of these creatures during the Cambrian period (541 to 485.4 million years ago) these creatures have had a significant impact on the levels of atmospheric carbon dioxide for the simple reason that they remove it from the atmosphere to make their shells. The fossil remains of once super-abundant forms such as brachiopods and ammonites make up vast beds of limestone and dolomite around the globe. Whole mountain ranges (including the Himalayas and Alps) are made up of these minerals. Furthermore, the seas were once filled with single-celled organisms called foraminifera whose calcium carbonate shells formed the vast beds of chalk that were deposited during the Cretaceous Period. The graph below demonstrates

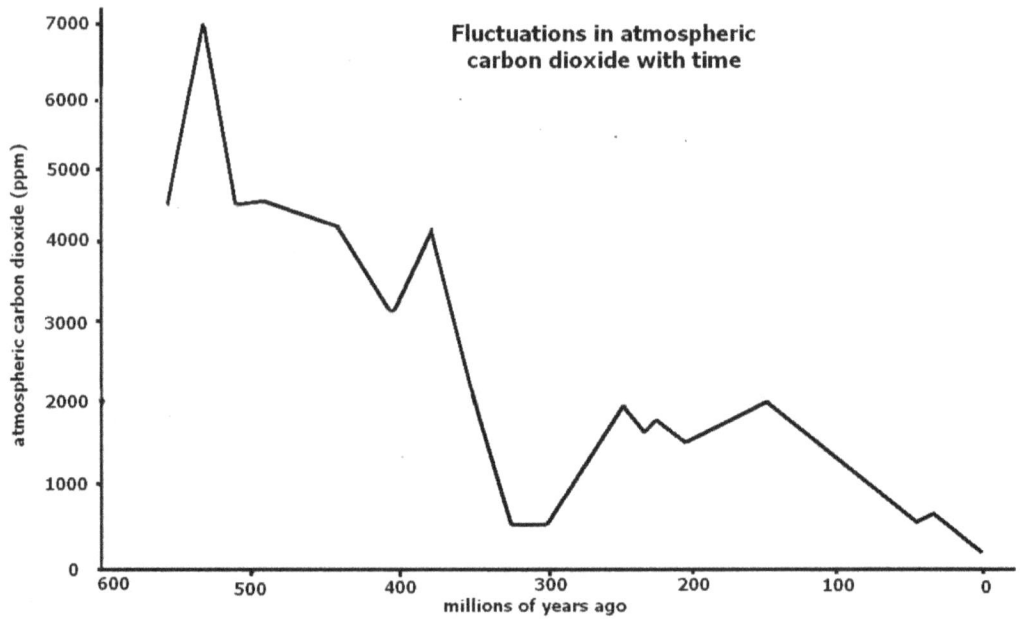

Plate 13: Prehistoric Atmospheric Carbon Dioxide Levels

the extent to which carbon dioxide was scrubbed from the atmosphere by these organisms, before ultimately being locked up in sedimentary rock layers.

The resultant dramatic drop in atmospheric carbon dioxide resulted in steady global cooling that may, in part, have been responsible for the most recent cycle of ice ages.

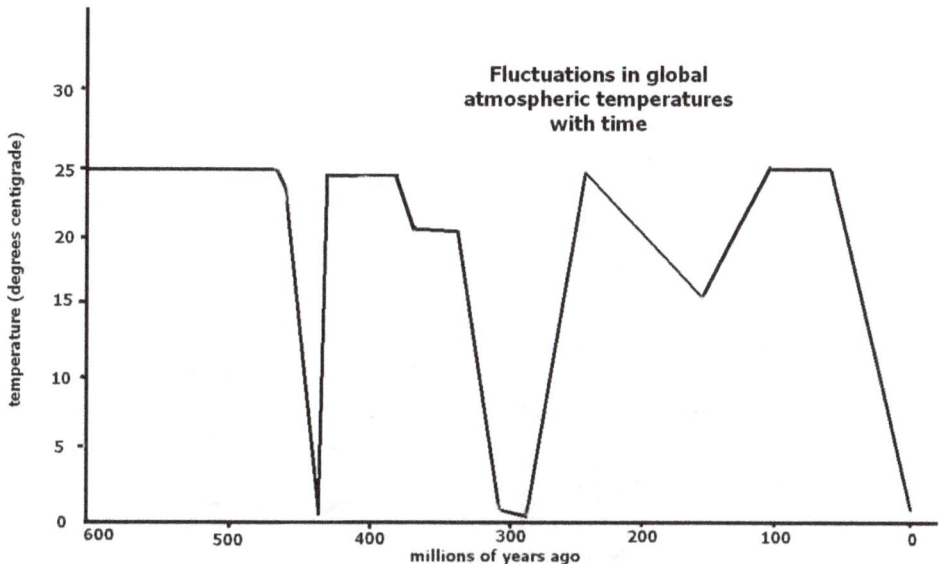

Plate 14: Prehistoric Atmospheric Temperatures

Following the end of the Cretaceous Period and the global cataclysm that brought about the extinction of around three quarters of the species on Earth, populations of marine molluscs and foraminifera declined to the current low levels. (Interestingly, hard corals experienced a rapid expansion at this time, utilising still more carbon dioxide to construct their skeletons) As a result of a natural process known as the rock cycle, the carbon dioxide trapped in fossil shells, foraminifera

THE CONSPIRACY CONSPIRACY

and corals is gradually being released into the atmosphere.

This is certainly a far greater factor in the increase of atmospheric CO_2 than is generally acknowledged.

$$CaCO_3 + 2H_2CO_3 \leftrightharpoons Ca(HCO_3)_2 + CO_2 + H_2O$$

Additionally, the subduction and heating of carbonate rocks during the movement of tectonic plates releases their carbon dioxide:

$$CaCO_3 \leftrightharpoons CaO + CO_2$$

Ultimately, as a result of these processes, all the vast deposits of carbon dioxide fixed in the shells of molluscs and foraminifera will re-enter the atmosphere – but there is still a long way to go!

Plate 15: Titchwell Beach Razor Shells

Hooray for technology!

Why on Earth should our government – most governments – wish to alarm the population with dire warnings of climatic collapse? The answer is implicit in Chomsky's 'Ten Strategies for Manipulation' referred to in the introduction. Having scared the pants off us all, the industrial-political complex announces that there are possible solutions available, but these will necessitate sacrifices on our part and dramatic changes in our life-styles. There is never any examination of the environmental impact of these alternatives, nor open discussion of the emissions for which they themselves are responsible.

- Alternative energy provision from solar panels and wind farms will replace traditional sources such as coal, oil, gas which generate carbon dioxide. *(No mention is ever made of how the high-tech metals and plastics are going to be made without vast consumption of electrical energy and hydrocarbons. The expected life span of an offshore wind turbine is variously quoted to be from 10 -20 years. Whichever is the case, the whole lot will require regular maintenance and replacement at some point.)*

- Petrol and diesel-fueled cars, lorries and public transport will be phased out, to be replaced by electrically-powered vehicles. *(Again: where will the electricity to supply charging points come from?*

THE CONSPIRACY CONSPIRACY

The production from wind and solar generation can never come close to providing enough. Additionally, many of the metals used in the large rechargeable batteries required are very scarce: there will never be enough of them to satisfy demand.)

- Additional nuclear power stations will be built to provide extra capacity. (*The fact that cement production is the second largest man-made source of carbon dioxide is never publicly acknowledged: large amounts are used during construction of a nuclear power station. And when did nuclear power suddenly become environmentally friendly? As more and more nations build them, who will undertake to process and store greatly increased amounts of nuclear waste? Who will ensure that hostile governments and terrorist groups cannot obtain it for use in 'dirty bombs'?)*

Conspiracy theory

The industrial-political complex has hijacked the largely natural phenomenon of global warming to achieve even greater control of the population and ever-larger revenue streams in sales of new technology and taxation.

- The Earth's climate is gradually rebounding from the last ice age, resulting in totally predictable and quantifiable warming of the oceans and atmosphere. This fact is concealed from the general public or buried among misleading and irrelevant propaganda.

- Taken in the context of the entire geological history of the planet, the present concentration of carbon dioxide in the atmosphere is close to an all-time low: graphs published to prove the opposite are carefully crafted to exaggerate the situation.

- This is also true of average global temperatures: aside from past ice ages, we are living through one of the *cooler* periods in Earth's history.

- The construction of wind and solar farms of debatable long-term value has made a lot of people a lot of money. By playing the global warming 'card', those in the industrial-political complex who have benefitted from the proliferation of these ugly structures have been allowed to proceed with only token resistance: this despite the fact that both have been shown to have had some very eco-unfriendly effects on wild life. Evidence of this is routinely suppressed, even by conservation charities.

- Reduction in the import of fossil hydrocarbons by western governments limits the political power of their main producers in the Middle East and Africa and reduces balance of payment deficits.

THE CONSPIRACY CONSPIRACY

- The destruction of the British coal industry largely contributed to the elimination of the Trade Unions, one of the few groups with sufficient political power to stand up to the government.

THE CONSPIRACY CONSPIRACY

Chapter 5: No more heroes...

WHO did you admire when you were a kid? Pop stars? Footballers? It probably depends on your age. Having been born in the early 1950s, many of my heroes were people who'd carried out incredible acts of skill and bravery in the Second World War. These included pilots like Eric 'Winkle' Brown, Douglas Bader, Leonard Cheshire and Guy Gibson.

Being a bit of a nerd, I also deeply admired pioneering scientists such as Mary Anning, Prof. R V Jones, Marie Curie, Frank Whittle, Francis Crick and James Watson. Of course, I had **some** sporting heroes, chief among them being Roger Bannister, Jimmy Greaves and Fred Trueman.

As far as I know all of the above deserved the admiration they received, but, in these days of cheque book journalism and rampant iconoclasm, fame tends to be very ephemeral. A chance remark to a friend at a party or

Plate 16: The author with Capt. Eric Brown

acquaintance can end up on the front page of the tabloids the next morning, while careers have been destroyed by ill-considered posts on the social media. I have to say, I fail to see how the public interest is served by revealing the thoughtless ramblings of an otherwise impeccably-behaved public servant at a private party, thereby bringing about the end of his or her career.

Today's young people might be surprised to be told that back in the early sixties, posters of politicians and radical political thinkers often featured alongside those of musicians and sporting personalities on the walls of bedrooms and college common rooms. Many teenagers followed the careers of public figures like John F Kennedy, Ernesto 'Che' Guevara and Martin Luther King with genuine enthusiasm and interest.

Even though I was only twelve at the time, I can still vividly remember the shocking impact of the assassination of John Kennedy. His cruel and very public death in November 1963 and the sight of his poor, beautiful wife attempting to retrieve fragments of his skull from the boot of the presidential Lincoln are images that defined a generation.

This iconic figure will be remembered by many people as the President who faced up to the Soviet leader Nikita Khrushchev, possibly preventing a nuclear war during the Cuban Missile Crisis. To some, he was the inspiration behind the American Apollo Program to land men on the Moon. Still others will remember Kennedy as the President who attempted to oppose the industrial-military complex,

THE CONSPIRACY CONSPIRACY

blocked the escalation of American involvement in South East Asia, constrained the power of both the mob **and** the CIA and began the emancipation of black Americans. It has been widely suggested by many that these were contributory factors to his assassination. In my opinion the evidence of a conspiracy at work in Dealey Plaza is beyond dispute. I shan't rehearse **all** the various theories, but a few less well-known facts are worth recording:

- Following his alleged part in the assassination of JFK, Lee Harvey Oswald reportedly walked several blocks, boarded a bus, before taking a taxi back to the boarding house where he lived. He then wandered off to the corner of 10th Street and Patton Avenue where, with no provocation, we are led to believe he gunned down Police Officer J.D. Tippitt. (First 'damned' fact: the shell cases retrieved at the scene were from a 38 **automatic** pistol: the gun carried by Oswald when he was arrested was an unfired, fully-loaded 38 revolver that used entirely different **flanged** rounds.)
- Oswald then **ran** the few blocks to Jefferson Avenue, where he entered a cinema, the Texas Theatre, **without paying!** Is this the action of a fugitive trying to remain inconspicuous? Given events in Dealey Plaza, the cashier, needless to say, called the police. (Second 'damned' fact: given the demands on Dallas' finest in and around the original crime

scene, why did the dispatcher immediately send perhaps as many as **thirty** officers to investigate someone suspected only of failing to pay for a cinema ticket? Why did Oswald calmly sit in the cinema until he was pointed out from the stage, almost as if he – and they – were working to a script?

- If you watch videos of the Presidential motorcade, you'll notice that the route involves negotiating a tight left hand bend onto Elm Street. (Third 'damned' fact: when the motorcade was planned somebody would **undoubtedly** have queried the choice of a route that necessitated slowing down to walking pace.)

- As the limousines slow down, you can see that the President's security guards are being instructed by a senior officer to dismount, leaving the President completely unprotected. One of them can be seen waving his arms in obvious frustration.

- Finally: the various videos and still photos taken just after the assassination show the majority of people in the Plaza looking towards the famous grassy knoll: others (including police officers) can be seen running towards the knoll and the picket fence behind it that is the perfect location for a lone sniper or one element of a crossfire team.

There is little doubt that some elements of Kennedy's

THE CONSPIRACY CONSPIRACY

private life left a bit to be desired: he almost certainly was involved with the glorious Marilyn Monroe and, with his brother, may even be implicated in her suspicious death. However, he does seem to have been the last President who intended to leave office having made the country better for all its citizens.

Some people hold the opinion that the line 'The day the music died' in Don McClean's haunting ballad 'American Pie' is an oblique reference to the assassination of JFK, his brother Robert and Dr Martin Luther King, (possibly referred to in the song as **"...the three men I admire most, The Father, Son and the Holy Ghost".**)

Whether true or not, this line seems a very accurate expression of the way things began to change after November 22nd, 1963. The age of heroism in public office gave way to iconoclasm, self-seeking and cynical abuse of executive power. As early as January 17th, 1961 outgoing US President and war hero Dwight D Eisenhower warned Americans:

"In the councils of government, we must guard against the acquisition of unwarranted influence, whether sought or unsought, by the military-industrial complex. The potential for the disastrous rise of misplaced power exists and will persist"

Despite this courageous statement, the abrupt termination of Kennedy's presidency was followed by that of Lyndon B Johnson who virtually agreed to everything he was told to do:

- Johnson allowed the 'police action' in Vietnam to escalate into a costly and bloody war that made billions for US arms manufacturers.
- The US space program was farmed out all over the United States: the Marshall Centre, The Jet Propulsion Laboratory, Edwards Airforce Base, Kennedy Space Centre and The Manned Spaceflight Center, which was constructed in Houston, Texas (LBJ's home state, which he served as Senator).
- The geographical dispersal of NASA facilities and their contractors was to prove costly, contributing greatly to logistical overheads and critical (and, in the case of the Challenger disaster, fatal) communication failures between Mission Control and the Cape.

Since the 1960s US Presidents seem to have become increasingly concerned with using their executive powers for their own financial gain and that of their supporters. It is possible to argue that the resistance Kennedy encountered throughout his presidency, his murder, and that of his brother (Attorney General and heir apparent Robert Kennedy) was intended as a warning from the military-industrial complex to subsequent Presidents.

History records that the terms of office of Nixon, Reagan, Clinton, the two Bushes and Trump were far from stain-free and included the rubber stamping of numerous military actions and acts of aggression, culminating in the costly (and probably illegal) 'Operation Iraqi Freedom'. The justification given for the invasion and eight and a half year occupation of Iraq was the alleged possession by the Iraqi armed forces of 'weapons of mass destruction' and the complicity of the country's leader, Saddam Hussein, in international terrorism. In fact no evidence was ever presented that Saddam was involved in the 911 attacks, nor in any covert or military action against states outside the Gulf region. Furthermore, despite minute scrutiny, independent inspectors failed to locate any evidence of weapons of mass destruction (ie: chemical and biological agents and nuclear devices).

To an impartial observer the whole 'War on Terror' has the look of an operation primarily intended to secure access to oil and gas supplies in the Middle East: although the actual figure is difficult to pin down, the US annually imports between 150 and 400 million barrels of Iraqi oil. Even the 2001 incursion into Afghanistan has been linked by some to US investment in the Trans-Afghanistan Gas Pipeline. However, whether hydrocarbons were a factor in these actions or not, huge sums of money are yet again being earned by US arms manufacturers.

There is a tragic irony in the fact that John F Kennedy is *still* criticized by many for the money he committed to the program for putting an American on the Moon. This cost the taxpayer a total of twenty three billion dollars, compared with the cost of the US involvement in Iraq and Afghanistan, estimated in 2017 at around **two and a half trillion dollars!**

THE CONSPIRACY CONSPIRACY

That would have paid for 1000 Apollo Programs! (A recent study at Harvard University suggested a figure of six trillion is more realistic.)

Conspiracy theory

- The assassination of President John F Kennedy was a coup d'etat, staged by the military-industrial complex to assert control over the government of the United States.

- Despite the many achievements of his short presidency, Kennedy's reputation has been cynically eroded with stories of links to organized crime and sexual incontinence. His two brothers (both of whom shared his political ambitions) were similarly attacked by the media.

- The majority of subsequent Presidents have furthered the ambitions of the Pentagon and powerful industrialists, in return for political and financial support.

- The arms industries of most industrial nations exert a dangerous and unwarranted influence over governments.

- Military leaders achieve high rank by demonstrating their ability to develop strategy and lead armed forces in battle. They do not share most people's abhorrence of warfare and many, in fact, relish it as a chance to test their tactical skills.

THE CONSPIRACY CONSPIRACY

- War, and preparation for it, has become the greatest budgeted expenditure of most nations on Earth. The slightest excuse is often sufficient to start a war: if no genuine justification exists, one can be fabricated.

- The real reasons for prosecuting any war are rarely given to the public: rather, they are misled with half truths, exaggerations and propaganda. Most people's understanding of international politics (or even geography!) is so basic that they readily believe what they are told by their leaders. (I wonder how many Britons could point on a globe to Kuwait, The Falklands or Afghanistan!)

THE CONSPIRACY CONSPIRACY

Chapter 6: The truth, the whole truth and anything but the truth!

IN the previous chapter I touched briefly upon the fact that some of history's defining events may not have been all they seemed and that hidden agendas may have lain behind the actions of political and spiritual leaders that remain undisclosed to this day.

I'd like to develop this further by re-examining three episodes that proved critical in the shaping of the modern world and considering whether the historical record truly is an accurate reflection of what occurred.

The 1936 Abdication Crisis

Even today, most people are familiar with the story of how Edward, the handsome playboy Prince of Wales, acceded to the throne in January, 1936, but abdicated in December the same year in favour of his younger brother, George (who would thus become Britain's wartime King three years later)

The usual simplistic reason given for Edward's actions is that he stepped down in order to marry the twice-divorced American heiress Wallis Simpson, it being put to him that it was politically and morally unacceptable for a King to be married to a woman with two living ex-husbands. The situation was chiefly precipitated by the Prime Minister, Stanley Baldwin, who made it plain that he and his government would resign if the marriage and coronation went ahead. This would have resulted in a general election and a very real threat to the throne: a constitutional monarchy can only function if it is politically neutral.

Having abdicated, Edward was given the title Duke of Windsor and married Mrs Simpson in June, 1937. Following the outbreak of World War 2, he was packed off to the Caribbean, with the minor office of Governor of the Bahamas.

But Princes of Wales and even Kings of England had behaved with far greater impropriety and disregard for convention in the past: Edward's grandfather and namesake Edward VII famously had a string of mistresses, his nine year reign being characterized by every possible excess. Despite (or perhaps because of) his vast appetite for alcohol, food and female company, Edward VII was a very popular monarch: much more so than his somewhat dour son, George. Could there be a hidden reason that the establishment was so keen to bring about the downfall and marginalization of Edward VIII?

At the time of George V's death in 1936, Great Britain was still attempting to recover from the social, economic and political turmoil of the First World War. The pointless slaughter of an entire generation had generated widespread republican reaction and the abolition of monarchies across the whole of Europe: many in Great Britain were keen to see the House of Windsor and hereditary aristocracy go the same way.

The rapid rise of the British Labour Movement in the aftermath of the Great War was seen as a very real threat to the British establishment, who feared anything that seemed likely to provoke the extreme political left into revolution. (This may be one of the reasons why details of the murder of Tsar Nicholas II of Russia and his family and George V's failure to offer the Romanovs sanctuary while it was still possible, was largely suppressed at the time.)

More than anything, it was probably the threat of revolution that brought about the redefining of the British Throne as a constitutional monarchy with only very limited and largely ceremonial powers.

So was Edward VIII's forced abdication precipitated by actions and opinions potentially far more inflammatory than marrying a divorcee?

It is not generally remembered that during the years leading up to the Second World War there was a very active and widely-supported Fascist party in Britain. Founded in 1932 by aristocrat Sir Oswald Moseley, 6th Baronet Ancoats, the British Union of Fascists included many influential and wealthy establishment figures among its supporters.

My father grew up in the East End of London and, in October 1936, witnessed first-hand the so-called 'Battle of Cable Street'. This was the confrontation between local

THE CONSPIRACY CONSPIRACY

people and Moseley's supporters, who were intending to march through a predominantly Jewish region of London. Up until this point Moseley's BUF had achieved a respectable following and, but for this miscalculation of public feelings, might have had an impact on negotiations with Germany and the stance taken by the British Government before the outbreak of World War 2. Certainly the support for the BFU among the general public largely evaporated after the Cable Street confrontation.

That is not to say, however, that this was entirely the case among the British aristocracy: the original membership of the fascist 'Right Club', formed in 1939 by MP Archibald Ramsay, included over 200 influential men and women, including many with titles.

The marriage of Oswald Moseley to Diana Mitford two days after the declaration of war created ties to several families close to both the throne and government. The fact that the ceremony took place in the house of Joseph Goebels (the Nazi's Chief of Propaganda) with Adolf Hitler as a guest suggests that the Nazi leadership were already aware of the potential value of support from the British ruling classes and were interested in discovering what possibilities might exist to in achieve it.

In fact as early as January 1936, Hitler received a telegram from the German Embassy in London stating that

"An alliance between Germany and Britain is for [Edward VIII] an urgent necessity."

THE CONSPIRACY CONSPIRACY

In the October following his abdication, Edward (now the Duke of Windsor) and his wife made an unofficial visit to Germany at the invitation of Hitler, being entertained by him at the Berghof. During their stay, the couple met most of the leading Nazis and even visited a concentration camp.

Since the end of the war, historical revisionists have consistently attempted to portray this visit (and one Edward had made earlier to meet with the Italian Fascist dictator Benito Mussolini) as, at worst, ill-judged and naïve and, at best, as assisting the government in their policy of appeasement. It is generally claimed that the Duke's real motive was to give Wallis a taste of the lifestyle that was denied to her by the government's refusal to allow her to adopt the title 'Her Royal Highness'. Royal biographer Andrew Morton, however, has stated that:

"[Edward] was certainly sympathetic... even after the war he thought Hitler was a good fellow and that he'd done a good job in Germany, and he was also anti-Semitic, before, during and after the war."

There is absolutely no question that The Duke of Windsor felt that peace between Germany and Britain could be achieved through negotiation and diplomacy: given the German ancestry of the House of Windsor, it is not difficult to believe that Edward hoped for a *detente* between the two nations that might ultimately result in them jointly becoming the two greatest imperial powers on Earth.

Furthermore, the advanced level of military readiness

THE CONSPIRACY CONSPIRACY

Edward witnessed on his visit to Germany in 1936 might have persuaded him that a second major conflict in twenty years would inevitably result in defeat, national bankruptcy and loss of empire.

Had the Nazis won the war, various scenarios have been suggested about the future employment of the Duke of Windsor in government. Following a British capitulation, he might have been invited to replace his brother George as King of England: whether he would have agreed to this or not, we'll never know, but the flight of Nazi Deputy Rudolf Hess to Scotland in an attempt to discuss a cessation of hostilities with members of the British aristocracy suggest the Nazis at least thought it might be a strong possibility. In August 1942, Edward's brother, the Duke of Kent, was killed when the Sunderland flying boat aboard which he was a passenger flew into a mountain in Scotland. Some reputable commentators have linked this event to a plot involving the Dukes of Windsor and Kent (both of whom were alleged to have pro-Nazi sympathies) with the attempt by Hess to broker a secret deal with British Intelligence and members of the Scottish aristocracy.

In my opinion Edward's open admiration for the German Nazi Party and its leader made him an embarrassment to the British Government. This could only be resolved with the collusion of the Church of England, and involved accusing him (with no legal precedent) of provoking a constitutional crisis because of his intention of marrying a divorcee.

THE CONSPIRACY CONSPIRACY

Even following the abdication, Edward still posed a very real threat, particularly after his visit to Germany in 1936. Still bitter following the circumstances surrounding the loss of his throne and seduced by promises of its return after a German victory:

- He could have been abducted by Nazi Commandos, flown to Germany and used for propaganda broadcasts.
- He might have agreed to work covertly to increase support for an end to fighting and the signing of a non-aggression treaty.

This necessitated his removal to the Bahamas, but even there he continued to make gloomy predictions about the inevitability of a Nazi victory. Following the eventual defeat of the Third Reich, The Duke and Duchess of Windsor went into virtual exile in France, being allowed to return to Britain (for family funerals) just twice before his death.

Every now and then the government releases state secrets under the 'thirty years rule', with the proviso that some eligible documents may be judged too sensitive for publication. At the moment, the release of the file on the abdication of Edward VIII and his connections with Nazi Germany have been deferred to the currently scheduled date of 2037.

It's probably not far off the truth to say that the popularity of Princes William and Harry and of their photogenic consorts has halted – or at least slowed – Britain's slide towards becoming a republic. Their father's somewhat outré beliefs, his admitted and very public infidelities and his treatment of their mother, Princess Diana, caused many to question his suitability for kingship: the record of his siblings in hardly better. The release of sensational revelations about the Nazi sympathies of Charles' uncle might easily be the straw that broke the proverbial camel's back...

The Cold War and the threat of nuclear holocaust

As I've mentioned above, I grew up in the 1950s just outside the east end of London. Even now, nearly seventy years later, I vividly remember how the threat of nuclear warfare hung over everyone like a black cloth.

Throughout my early life I recall that it was assumed by most people that nuclear war was both unavoidable and imminent: I sometimes reflect on the psychological impact this must have had on children. At the school I attended we carried out occasional 'duck and cover' drills (although I don't think many of us really understood why we were rolled up under our desks), while the familiar sound of air raid sirens being tested punctuated our lessons and playtimes. (I wonder if they would have been used in the event of a real nuclear attack: after all, what could people actually **do** in the four minutes after a warning – boil an egg?)

The Cuban Missile Crisis occurred when I was eleven years old: so serious was the threat of nuclear war that I can honestly remember my mother and father saying goodbye rather than goodnight to my brother and me when we went to bed!

Briefly: the crisis was precipitated when, in October 1962, American U2 spy planes photographed the installation of Soviet missile sites on the island of Cuba, just 60 miles from the American mainland. Further overflights suggested that 8,000 Soviet troops were deployed in Cuba (in fact the true figure is now known to have been 40,000+) and that the bases were intended to house ballistic missiles that could have been targeted on most American cities. The United States put in place a naval blockade in an attempt to prevent Soviet cargo ships from delivering further missiles, which was seen as a serious provocation by the Soviet leadership. Premier Nikita Khrushchev threatened all kinds of dire consequences and the world held its breath as the ships approached the picket line. In the event both sides drew back from the brink of war: on October 28th, Khrushchev ordered the missiles to be removed, while Kennedy secretly agreed not to invade Cuba and to withdraw Thor IRBMs from Turkey.

The Cuban Missile Crisis is generally seen as the 'hottest' incident in the Cold War (the undeclared state of hostilities between the Soviet Union and its Warsaw Pact allies and the member states of NATO) In fact it was probably just one of thousands of similar flash points, many of which went unrecorded. 'War by Proxy' in Korea, Vietnam and the Middle East could, in theory, have easily escalated into super-power conflicts, while it is now conceded that literally

THE CONSPIRACY CONSPIRACY

hundreds of 'high alert states' were triggered by straying civil aircraft, software failures, misinterpreted military training manoeuvres and a host of other innocent factors.

How did this mistrust between former World War 2 allies begin? And did the Soviet Union **really** seek world domination as countless films and novels suggest?

The German invasion of the Soviet Union that commenced in June, 1941 probably resulted in the deaths of as many as twenty million Russians. Perhaps 200,000 of these were killed by Soviet 'Barrier Troops' (veterans placed in the second line of a battle to prevent retreat by the less-experienced front line) while between five and six million were killed as a result of Stalin's draconian racial policies. (For example, the Katyn massacre of 1940, when 22,000 Polish Army and Police officers were murdered by the by the Soviet NKVD ("People's Commissariat for Internal Affairs") A further half a million dissidents and intellectuals died in Stalin's forced labour Gulags.

Few details of this emerged until after the end of war, for the simple reason that 'Operation Barbarossa' had caused Stalin's transformation from an Axis partner of Hitler to an unlikely member of the Allies. When it became obvious that the Soviet armies were **not** going to be withdrawn from the countries they had 'liberated' during the defeat of the Third Reich, the Soviet leadership and Communism as a philosophy began to be portrayed by the western powers in an entirely different light. For example, the rape of as

THE CONSPIRACY CONSPIRACY

many as two million German women was disclosed, as were the pre-war atrocities committed by the Russians in satellite states like the Ukraine.

The Cold War began with a perceived need by the Allied powers to maintain a military presence in mainland Europe to oppose the forces of the Warsaw Pact and by the Soviets in justification for establishing a **cordon sanitaire** around their western borders.

It is possible to view this with a certain degree of sympathy: Russia had been attacked without provocation on numerous occasions, most notably by the forces of Napoleon, the Kaiser, Adolf Hitler and even the Japanese (in 1904) These chapters in Soviet history had proven costly, both financially and in terms of human life: more significantly, they also scarred the psyche of the Soviet leadership. It became implicit in foreign policy that no enemy army would cross the borders without a response that involved the commitment of the entire population, whatever the cost.

This transparently hostile foreign policy was first highlighted by wartime leader Winston Churchill in his famous Fulton, Missouri speech of March 1946:

"From Stettin in the Baltic to Trieste in the Adriatic, an iron curtain has descended across the continent."

With Europe divided into two armed camps and the world encouraged by propaganda and financial aid to take sides with NATO or the Warsaw Pact, the global industrial-military complex seized the opportunity to increase peacetime arms spending to the levels it had enjoyed during the Second World War. In the period 1947 – 1950 annual military spending in the US expenditure never exceeded $60 billion: after 1952, it never fell below $140 billion!

Did the Soviet Union really have ambitions to defeat the west militarily? Or were the establishment of puppet satellite states, the building of the Berlin Wall and the arms race primarily defensive? And has the United States been the custodian of world peace for seventy years or are there much baser motives behind its foreign policy?

The quote below is from a Latvian man was in response to a BBC request for personal experiences of the Cold War: it displays succinctly how ordinary people on both sides of the Iron Curtain were swayed by state propaganda:

I grew up during Cold War in USSR. My childhood wish was for The Atomic War not to happen and as I went to bed I thanked destiny (God was forbidden) that I was not born in U.S.A. or England where "kids were suffering". Only after Perestroika and independence (Latvia is a EU member now), I understood to what extent [the] propaganda machine washed brains of millions of people. Nothing better than image of The Enemy for dictatorship: much like what's happening now in Russia...

An impartial observer (who would probably need to have originated on another planet!) might well consider that the demonization of communism during the US McCarthy era (when nobody with liberal attitudes was safe from being labelled un-American) and the Soviet antipathy to capitalist democracy were as illogical and hysterical as each other. Neither philosophy seems to have achieved any lasting happiness or security for the proletariat: both have resulted in wealthy oligarchies where just a tiny minority enjoy wealth and power.

All those years of fearful anticipation, the billions spent on cold war bases, bunkers and control centres and the pointless slaughter of millions of civilians and combatants in the endless succession of 'cold war actions' may ultimately be viewed as the price paid by the many to further the ambitions of the few. Looking back on the era of 'Mutually Assured Destruction', would anyone have ever 'pressed the button' that wiped out mankind except by accident? With hindsight, I really doubt it; it wouldn't have been good for business!

The Space Race

Future generations may well view the period from 1957 to 1972 as one of the defining eras in scientific advancement. I often reflect that my late father was born in 1919, the year in which Alcock and Brown first flew the Atlantic: fifty years later he and I sat in front of the television watching the first humans walking on the Moon (Allegedly!) What an incredible rate of change for his generation to come to terms with!

My interests in spaceflight, Astronomy and aviation all basically stem from the launch in October 1957 of Sputnik 1,

THE CONSPIRACY CONSPIRACY

the world's first artificial satellite. The fact that the Soviet Union had the knowledge and technical competence to achieve this first came as a shock to the scientists trying to achieve the same result with the US Navy's Vanguard program. The following year a Juno rocket (hurriedly adapted from a Jupiter C IRBM from the Army's nuclear inventory) responded in kind with the launch of the tiny (13kg) Explorer 1. The race was on!

The dent to national pride was intolerable to the American public, who took some consolation from the often-repeated (and wrongly-attributed) statement that:

'Their Germans are better than our Germans'

This is a reference to the fact that at the end of World War Two there was a desperate free-for-all between the occupying powers to acquire the scientists and technologies behind Germany's incredibly innovative jet and rocket programs. In fact, the cream of the crop decided to surrender to the United States, who they rightly thought would treat them as valuable enough to ignore their Nazi affiliations. These recruits included Wernher Von Braun, Ernst Stuhlinger, Konrad Dannenberg, Walter Dornberger and Guenter Wendt, all of whom played significant roles in post-war US aerospace.

The Russian harvest did include **some** leading German rocket scientists, chief among whom was Helmut Gröttrup, who assisted chief of the Soviet space program Sergei Korolev in the design of the R1 missile. (It is conveniently forgotten in the west that before the war, Russia was at least as advanced as Germany in rocket theory and design.)

THE CONSPIRACY CONSPIRACY

Just as we have seen in the section preceding this, the American public were encouraged to believe that the Soviet space program posed a threat to the security of the United States. The fear that nuclear weapons could be delivered from orbiting satellites (in minutes rather than the hours a fleet of bomber aircraft would require) was used as a lever to generate ever-increasing expenditure on missile programs.

The development of much more powerful rocket motors gave intercontinental range to the next generation of missiles: at the time no defence against an incoming ICBM warhead existed, so the use of orbiting weapons became largely irrelevant.

This development could have brought an end to the launching of increasingly heavy and complex satellites of little perceived military value. Similarly, the ambitions of both sides to launch human beings into space would have required vast amounts of money to achieve. The answer was The Space Race. The American public (by nature generally competitive and patriotic) was easily persuaded to forget the initial fear of a potential military use of space by the Soviets. Instead it became a matter of national pride to catch up with the Soviets and beat them to their future goals. Undoubtedly the same was true in the Soviet Union, where it must have been quite a challenge to persuade people still queuing for rationed bread that it was worth spending billions of rubles to put a dog into space!

THE CONSPIRACY CONSPIRACY

In April, 1961 the Soviet Union scored the opening points when Yuri Gagarin became the first human space traveller (or Cosmonaut, as the Soviets call them) At the time the Americans were struggling to achieve reliability with the Atlas missile that was intended to launch Mercury spacecraft into orbit: as a stop-gap, a Redstone IRBM was hurriedly adapted to launch the Mercury capsule for a fifteen minute sub-orbital mission. To say the US public was unimpressed by the first two Mercury-Redstone missions is an understatement! Although Alan Shepard and 'Gus' Grissom (his actual fore-name was Ivan!) were feted like true American heroes, their 110-mile hops were widely dismissed as 'competition in spirit rather than practice'

In 1962 Marine Pilot John Glenn became the first American Astronaut to orbit the Earth: following his safe return he experienced levels of adulation that are unlikely to be repeated. But just seven months after this first successful US orbital mission, President John Kennedy had made an astonishing promise that an American would walk on the Moon before the end of the decade!

There followed six years of triumph and tragedy on both sides of the Iron Curtain, which demonstrated that extreme danger is implicit in extraordinarily complex technology. Between them the United States and Soviet Union lost four men who would very probably have taken part in their respective countries attempted Moon landings.

THE CONSPIRACY CONSPIRACY

The deaths of Astronauts Chaffee, Grissom and White in a disastrous launch pad fire necessitated a complete redesign of the Apollo capsule's hatch, electrical system and oxygen supply. Astonishingly, NASA nevertheless managed to honour Kennedy's pledge with the launch of Apollo 11 in July 1969.

Even before the end of the Apollo Program three years later, doubts were being raised as to whether the grainy, low-resolution videos of the Apollo 11 mission were really filmed on the Moon. Photographic experts came forward to question the authenticity of the stills images, and comment upon the unexpectedly high standards of focus, framing and composition achieved by astronauts wearing clumsy, inflexible EVA gloves. As the complexity of the missions increased, growing numbers of people began to question the virtually flawless record of the Saturn V launch rocket and the Apollo spacecraft. Even on the Apollo 13 mission, when an explosion in cislunar space wrecked the service module that supplied power and oxygen, the crew miraculously survived. I have been fortunate enough to spend time with fourteen Apollo astronauts, six of whom were Moonwalkers. Over time I became increasingly aware of worrying discrepancies and scientific impossibilities in their accounts. Despite my enthusiasm for everything to do with astronautics, I was forced to conclude that the Moon landings had never taken place. I eventually wrote a gratifyingly well-received book ('Our Forbidden Moon') expressing my concerns, which I therefore won't repeat in any detail here. Suffice it to say:

THE CONSPIRACY CONSPIRACY

every single piece of evidence that is invoked as proof of the Moon landings can easily be dismissed. (Some of the main points can be found in an appendix at the end of this book.

To sum up:

- From its earliest days the Space Race became a central feature of the political rivalry between the Soviet Union and the United States and was an important element of their propaganda.

- The space programs of both the Soviet Union and the US suffered equipment malfunctions and loss of life, but only the United States adopted a policy of total transparency, televising all their manned launches worldwide.

- As a result, every achievement claimed by NASA was accepted enthusiastically and without question.

- Throughout the Gemini and Apollo programs numerous mission-threatening failures occurred, but (except in the case of the Apollo 1 fire) these were always 'resolved by the skill and quick-thinking of the Astronauts and mission controllers.'

- The apparent success of the six Moon landings gave a worldwide boost to the reputation and prestige of the United States and provided a distraction from its conduct of the Vietnam War.

THE CONSPIRACY CONSPIRACY

Conspiracy theory

- World events are frequently interpreted and reported for political and commercial advantage.

- Because a depressingly large percentage of the population lack any degree of critical discernment, they readily believe whatever they read in the newspaper, see on TV or come across in the social media.

- This makes it easy for whoever controls the media to shape public opinion, whether to affect the result of a referendum, gain support for an illegal war or destroy the reputation of a public figure, for example.

- Many people base their opinions upon the frequently conflicting outputs of papers like the Daily Mail and Guardian, while failing to realise that both cannot be reporting accurate accounts of the same news story.

- UK newspapers and online news services are currently owned by just seven groups. The largest share of the industry is held by two individuals, who between them control over 50%. Historically, the support of all of these publications has been given to whichever political party most closely reflects the interests of the owners: if party manifestos change, press allegiances change.

THE CONSPIRACY CONSPIRACY

Rupert Murdoch	**27.9%**
Lord Rothermere	**27.8%**
Trinity Mirror plc	**13.9%**
Alexander and Evgeny Lebedev	**10.1%**
Richard Desmond	**9.2%**
David and Frederick Barclay	**5.1%**
Scott Trust	**4.7%**
Pearson plc	**1.5%**

- Despite legislation such as the UK 2000 Freedom of Information Act, the government blocks the release of any material it decides is too sensitive, often without explanation. Additionally what *is* released is frequently incomplete or redacted. Below is a page from the Chilcot Report on the Iraq War: the testimony of Sir Richard Dearlove, the Head of MI6 at the time, has been so heavily censored that on most pages not a single word is legible!

Plate 17: Redacted document

Chapter 7: Don't shoot the messenger!

WHILE I am writing my books I occasionally reflect how fortunate I am to be an absolute non-entity! I'm self employed, own the company that publishes my output and my friends generally already consider me to be slightly eccentric in my beliefs! Although being the UK's only full-time meteorite dealer and a well-known blogger has given me a strong online presence, I'm unlikely to become of interest to the establishment or the intelligence community. I do, however, have personal experience of how refusing to toe the 'party line' can affect your career.

When I left teaching to become a full-time meteorite dealer and author, I occasionally accepted offers of supply work in a number of Norfolk High Schools. After a couple of happy years I was asked by the Head of Science at one of them to accompany a group of Year 9 students to the cinema, where a screening of Al Gore's film 'An Inconvenient Truth' had been arranged. To the HoD's surprise, I said that I'd rather not. When he asked to know my reasons, I explained that I had serious doubts about many of the film's core pieces of 'evidence'. I explained that the claims in the film that the melting of the snow on Mount Kilimanjaro, the predicted disastrous blocking of the Gulf Stream and the causes of Hurricane Katrina had all been discounted by impartial scientists. I suggested that it wasn't our role as teachers to expose pupils to wildly inaccurate propaganda. (Subsequently, courts on both sides of the Atlantic ruled that showing the film to school pupils without identifying it as a one-sided, politically motivated production with nine completely untrue central 'proofs' of global warming was in breach of educational legislation. How's **that** for an 'inconvenient truth'?)

Regardless, at the end of the day I was told my future services would no longer be required. Shortly afterwards the 'phone stopped ringing and my 35-year career in teaching came to an end! This had little or no impact on me personally, since my very modest financial needs were pretty much guaranteed by then. (As comedian Max Miller remarked when told by impresario Val Parnell that he would never work at the Palladium again: "Sorry Val – you're £80,000 too late!")

Others, however, have not been so fortunate: here are some of their stories...

Dr David Bellamy

There was a time when this entertaining and flamboyant character was the media's 'go-to' biologist. He was frequently invited to take part in natural history broadcasts and he was also a regular contributor to TV and radio chat shows, panel games and other light entertainment programs. He also presented numerous series of his own, including *Bellamy on Botany*, *Bellamy's Britain*, *Bellamy's Europe* and *Bellamy's Backyard Safari*.

Things began to slide for Dr Bellamy following his 1996 appearance on the BBC children's program 'Blue Peter', when he spoke out against the construction of wind farms in undeveloped rural sites. In 1997 he stood against the then Prime Minister, John Major, in a General Election and believes that his comments during this campaign were directly responsible for his abrupt decline as a media personality. His increasing skepticism about some of the published data on global warming and its causes (he wrote a much-quoted newspaper article in 2004 in which he described anthropogenic global warming as 'poppycock') led to him being replaced as President of the Royal Society of Wildlife Trusts the following year.

At the time (and still today to some extent) Dr Bellamy's intellectual abilities and academic qualifications were frequently minimized by the climate change lobby. He was referred to as a 'self-proclaimed expert' , an 'ex-laboratory technician' and an 'ill-informed eccentric'. Now forgive me if I'm being naïve, but isn't the scientific method supposed to be about the rational consideration of **all** the evidence? Shouldn't the opinion of a university lecturer in Botany count for as much (if not more) than that of a politician or 'hobby environmentalist'?

It is impossible to construe Bellamy's sudden fall from favour as anything other than the orchestrated silencing of the contrary opinions of a high-profile, highly qualified Scientist.

David Icke

Anyone who has ever attended a talk by David Icke or watched the many recorded videos available online will almost certainly concede that he is a skilled and passionate lecturer. He holds his large audiences spellbound for hours on end and every venue on his frequent world tours rapidly sells out. Since he changed career from sports journalist and commentator to professional lecturer, all but his most outré ideas have been shown to have some basis in fact. For years he has warned his audiences and readers of his many well-crafted books about the erosion of personal liberties, invasive surveillance, widespread institutionalised paedophilia, misuse of political, religious and economic power and the existence of secret elite groups that control every aspect of our lives. And yet he is still widely represented in the media as a deluded paranoiac who believes the Queen to be a shape-shifting reptilian alien.

Icke himself likes to quote a saying of MK 'Mahatma' Gandhi:

'First they ignore you, then they laugh at you, then they fight you, then you win.'

THE CONSPIRACY CONSPIRACY

Icke has certainly experienced three of these! One of his first – and last! – appearances as a 'conspiracy theorist' on TV was on the Wogan Show in 1991. When Wogan asked Icke why he, an ex-footballer and sports presenter, had been selected by God as the "chosen one", he replied that people would have said the same about Jesus: 'Who the heck are you? You're a carpenter's son." I can see no evidence of delusion or paranoia whatsoever in this response. It seems to me that Icke was making the point that even people from ordinary backgrounds are capable of extraordinary insights. He went on to try and explain to Wogan (an ex bank clerk!) that he believed all humans are inspired by God and can be conduits for divine communication. But of course, the BBC's 'National Treasure' rolled his eyes and went for cheap laughs. Icke himself has said that more than anything, this interview destroyed any hopes of early public acceptance of his ideas. (One has to question by what authority this buffoon of an Irish disc jockey was allowed to assassinate a sensitive human being's character so publicly.

It seems ironic that Wogan's chat show and charity work (for many years he was the only celebrity who received a fee for 'Children in Need') earned him a knighthood, UK citizenship, a memorial service at Westminster Abbey and a large house at Taplow, while Icke has been widely criticised for earning his living by trying to make the world a safer and fairer place.

THE CONSPIRACY CONSPIRACY

Bart Sibrel

There is little doubt that this former taxi driver genuinely believes that no human beings have visited the Moon: he has produced four films to present his interpretation of the NASA evidence that 'proves' they have.

The main thing Sibrel is remembered for, however, is being punched in the jaw while attempting to persuade Apollo 11 astronaut Buzz Aldrin to swear on the Bible that he really had walked on the Moon. Now whatever your opinion about Sibrel's claims, surely Aldrin was guilty of assault? In the same vein, the son of Dr Edgar Mitchell said he would call the CIA to have Sibrel 'waxed' and John Young threatened to punch him in the head!

If you look up Sibrel's biographical details on a well-known online encyclopedia, you'll find a number of examples of dismissive schoolboy-type comments. His videos (which have been viewed and enjoyed by millions) are described as '... **four amateurish films'.** His account of how he obtained some intriguing video clips is disputed with absolutely no evidence to the contrary, while space enthusiast Jim McDade's description of Sibrel's film ' **A Funny Thing Happened on the Way to the Moon'** as "...full of falsehoods, innuendo, strident accusations, half-truths, flawed logic and premature conclusions." is published unchallenged.

Possibly the most infamous item in this generally shoddy piece of journalism is, however, the paragraph that **with**

no relevance whatsoever describes a prosecution for vandalism brought against Sebril for an incident during a parking dispute. What does this have to do with **anything**?

When you consider the strange behaviour of a number of the twelve 'Moonwalkers' and six Command Module Pilots, following their alleged lunar missions (starting their own religious groups, searching for Noah's Ark, refusing to display any Apollo-related artefacts in their homes and so on) you begin to see that researchers like Bart Sibrel play an important and necessary role in the history of science: without them all kinds of claims can pass unchecked into orthodoxy.

In this context, I like to remember the maxim:

'Extraordinary claims require extraordinary proof'.

THE CONSPIRACY CONSPIRACY

Chapter 8: Conspiracy theories that refuse to go away

THE Internet is filled with websites devoted to innumerable 'conspiracy theories', as are the shelves of libraries and bookshops. Many – perhaps most – of these are ill-conceived, poorly-argued and based on very spurious evidence. The existence of these is of great advantage to those who attempt to ridicule genuine examples of politicians, military leaders and industrialists manipulating world events to their own advantage. From among the many, I've chosen a few that appear to have at least some element of truth:

The 911 attacks

On a recent anniversary of the attacks on the World Trade Centre and Pentagon in September, 2001, there was a documentary on British TV that presented *yet another* 'compelling scientific explanation' of how two modern steel-framed skyscrapers could collapse just a couple of hours after being struck by airliners. This new theory was required because there is still no consensus as to what caused the steel frames to melt:

THE CONSPIRACY CONSPIRACY

- The girders were thermally insulated and most fire-protection engineers dismiss the idea that the original impact could have stripped the insulation from the steel support-pillars.
- The jet fuel burned off very rapidly, limiting the temperature inside the towers to less than the melting point of steel.
- Three explosions were heard by over a hundred individual firefighters just before each of the towers collapsed.
- Many tall buildings have burned fiercely for far longer than WTC 1, 2 & 7 and not collapsed (In Madrid, Dubai, Chechnya and, in London, Grenfell Tower).

The two self-styled experts who presented the theory (one a chemist, one an aluminium smelter) claimed that the aircraft fuselages survived the impact and entered the centre of each tower in substantial-sized pieces: these melted and reacted with the '...vast amounts of water' (not vast enough to put out the burning office fittings, apparently!) to produce hydrogen, which exploded:

$2Al + 6H_2O = 2Al(OH)_3 + 3H_2$.

Problems with this theory:

- The report of the National Institute of Standards and Technology (NIST) is adamant that the planes were shredded into tiny pieces by the impact which could not have produced a sufficient quantity of

molten aluminium to cause an explosion (If this were not the case – if the planes survived as a few major chunks – then why did this not occur at the Pentagon, where few traces of wings, fuselage, etc. were recovered?)
- Why have the Port Authority (who hold the remaining WTC debris) refused to allow it to be examined for aluminium globules?
- Why, then, did WTC7 collapse *even though it had not been struck by an aircraft*? Explosions were seen and heard here, also.

The passage of time has failed to produce any compelling new evidence to dispel the widely-held belief that the attacks on the World Trade Centres and Pentagon were **not** carried out by fanatical Muslim terrorists, but rather were undertaken by elements within the United States military, intelligence community and government. In fact the opposite is true: there is an increasing body of evidence and testimony that undermines the official version of events. There are literally thousands of web-pages, books and videos out there concerned with the events of September 11th, 2001, so I'll restrict myself here to listing just a few of the more bizarre elements of the attack and its aftermath:
- Very conveniently, four of the claimed attackers' passports were recovered: that of Satam al Suqami was picked up on the street near the WTC by a passerby, two more were found in the debris field

THE CONSPIRACY CONSPIRACY

of hijacked United Airlines Flight 93 that crashed in Pennsylvania, while an examination of the luggage of attack-leader Mohamed Atta produced not just the passport of Abdulaziz Alomari, but also contained the names and biographical details of all nineteen men allegedly involved in the plot.

- There are several strange things about the collapse of WTC7, the third building in the complex to be destroyed. Firstly, it wasn't struck by any significant debris or fuel from the hijacked airliners, nor, apparently, did it burn with any particular ferocity: yet despite this and the efforts of large numbers of fire officers, it collapsed seven hours after WTC1 & 2. BBC Reporter Jane Standley announced the collapse in a live 'piece to camera' twenty three minutes before it actually occurred! WTC7 can plainly be seen behind Ms Standley during the broadcast. When members of the public requested copies of the video, A BBC spokesperson stated: ***"We no longer have the original tapes of our 9/11 coverage (for reasons of cock-up, not conspiracy). So if someone has got a recording of our output, I'd love to get hold of it. We do have the tapes for our sister channel News 24, but they don't help clear up the issue one way or another.***

More recently, a report by from the University of Alaska, Fairbanks, concluded that the WTC7 fire could not have brought the tower down. Dr J Leroy Hulsey, Chair of UAF's Civil and Environmental Engineering Department, revealed the findings at the Justice In Focus Symposium in New York in 2017. He said: ***"It is our preliminary conclusion based, upon our work to date, that fire did not produce the failure at this particular building."***

It may well be significant that WTC7 contained several floors of offices belonging to the US Secret Service, the CIA, and the Mayor's Office of Security Management. (Somewhat strangely, Mayor Guiliani and his team did not occupy this specially designed bunker on the day of the attack!)

- Just one more! At any crime scene, it is customary for all material evidence to be collected and retained for subsequent examination. This is also the case with train and aircraft disasters: the debris from the Columbia Shuttle break-up, for example, is stored in the VAB at the Kennedy Space Centre. Astonishingly, this was not the case with most of the steelwork from the World Trade Centre, which was rapidly sent for recycling at three US plants as well as others in India and China. There has been a good deal of scientific opinion suggesting that the 'gravitational collapse' of the three WTC towers could only have resulted from the use of super-thermite charges to cut steel beams and columns:

orange streams of molten metal seen falling from the towers has been categorically stated to be molten iron, a product of the thermite reaction. The destruction of the majority of the recovered steelwork (and the careful selection of samples sent for study by FEMA) has prevented a concerted examination of this possibility.

I'm not actively involved in researching the so-called 9/11 Conspiracy, but I'm certain of one thing: until the media and government stop dreaming up easily-dismissed new 'explanations' in response to ongoing investigation by those who **are**, the 911 attacks will continue to be seen by many as a cynical false flag operation intended to justify military action in the Middle East and Afghanistan. But would the US Government lie to its citizens and kill thousands of them in order to achieve a political goal? Sending troops into Iraq and Vietnam for entirely spurious reasons would suggest they might!

The death of Princess Diana

Let me start by saying straight away that my personal belief is that Diana, Princess of Wales, was killed as a result of some very reckless driving by Henri Paul, Deputy Head of Security at the Hôtel Ritz, Paris: I seriously doubt that the Royal Family or British intelligence services were involved in the planning or execution of a plot to kill Diana, but that is **not** to say that the crash of her Mercedes S-280 in the Pont de l'Alma Tunnel wasn't quickly seen by some as an opportunity that was too good to miss!

THE CONSPIRACY CONSPIRACY

Dozens of theories concerning the circumstances of the death of Diana and male companion 'Dodi' al Fayed have appeared over the years, ranging from the highly credible to the totally fantastic. Some of the more dramatic claims were made by al Fayed's father, billionaire Mohamed al Fayed, who still contends that Diana was pregnant with his son's child, that the pair were secretly engaged to be married and that they were killed by the security services to prevent the Princess (mother of the future King of England) from marrying a Muslim. Al Fayed further claimed that the 'murder' was carried out on the orders of Prince Philip. Not surprisingly, the Royal Family removed their warrant from Harrod's (al Fayed's Knightsbridge department store) in 2000: he subsequently sold the business to a Qatari consortium for a reported sum of £1.5 billion.

Al Fayed has been unable to present any proof whatsoever for his allegations and many elements of his story can readily be disproven:

- Had the Princess intended marrying Dodi al Fayed, she would most certainly have shared the fact with her close friends: she didn't, telling them instead that she '...needed another marriage like a rash on the face'.
- An autopsy did not specifically discount the possibility of Diana being pregnant, but al Fayed himself is the only person to suggest that she was. (He claimed the Princess had phoned him with the news half an hour before her death.) Several of her friends

stated that Diana was taking oral contraceptives and had just finished her period.
- It is hard to see why MI5 would have chosen an underpowered Fiat Uno to pursue the Princess's Mercedes and force its driver to lose control by the use of a super-powerful strobe light.

A sober consideration of the facts leads to the conclusion that the accident resulted from Henri de Paul driving at twice the speed limit in order to escape the attention of a gaggle of pursuing *paparazzi*. De Paul was Deputy Head of Security at the Ritz, not a professional chauffeur: he was described at the enquiry into the accident as '...probably a very nice man, but shit as a driver." There is some dispute about whether de Paul had been drinking before the crash: numerous security professionals have testified that Dodi's bodyguard would never have allowed DePaul to take the wheel if he had. Regardless, it seems apparent that the Frenchman misjudged his own competence to take part in a high speed car chase at night.

Despite the main elements of the 'Princess Diana Conspiracy' being adequately explained, there are still a great many people who feel that everything worked out just too conveniently for the British establishment.

Psychologists have identified a general need for great events to have great causes: being told that the dramatic death of 'The Princess of Hearts' was the result of bad driving seems too trivial for many to accept.

THE CONSPIRACY CONSPIRACY

But there is another aspect of the death of Princess Diana that has never been satisfactorily explained and which continues to generate speculation: events **after** the crash in the Alma tunnel.

Serious doubts have been expressed concerning the timing of episodes leading up to Diana's death. Here, as far as can be reliably established is a chronology of the events of the early morning of August 31st, 1997:

00.20: The Mercedes S-280 containing the Princess, Dodi al Fayed, his bodyguard Trevor Rees and Security Chief Henri de Paul leaves the Ritz Hotel, Paris.

00.25: The car, pursued by at least two *paparazzi* on motorcycles, crashes into a pillar in the Pont de l'Alma Tunnel at approximately 65mph.

00.26: Doctor Frederic Mailliez 'just happens' to be passing: he stops to examine the scene of the accident, quickly calling the emergency services. He discovers that de Paul and Dodi al Fayed are dead, but that Diana and Trevor Rees are still alive: the Princess is conscious and capable of speaking. He claims not to have recognized Diana.

00.28: Police arrive, cordon off the tunnel and begin rounding up paparazzi: eight are arrested.

00.32: A fire engine and several ambulances arrive on the scene.

01.25: **An hour after the crash** (having already been resuscitated following a cardiac arrest) Diana is placed in an ambulance to be driven to hospital.

THE CONSPIRACY CONSPIRACY

01.55: The ambulance stops so that adrenaline can be administered to the Princess.

02.06: The ambulance arrives at Pitie-Salpetriere Hospital **nearly an hour and three quarters after the accident.**

04.00: Princess Diana is declared dead.

This agreed timeline and its interpretation are the root and branch of all current 'conspiracy theories' about Diana's death. These are the main questions that many people feel require more convincing answers:

- Why did Dr Mailliez fail to recognize Diana? If he had, surely priority action such as calling for an air ambulance would have been taken.
- If (as was claimed later) Diana had a fist-sized tear in her pulmonary vein, why was she conscious when first examined by Dr Mailliez and why did it take her over three hours to die?
- Why did the Jean-Marc Martino, the onboard doctor of the ambulance, spend forty minutes fruitlessly trying to stabilize Diana's condition if he already suspected internal bleeding?
- Why did the ambulance not go to the nearest hospital (the Hotel-Dieu) rather than the Pitie-Salpetriere?
- When it finally left the accident scene, why did the ambulance travel as slowly as it did (reportedly less than 30mph) and make a five minute stop just as it was approaching the hospital?

Responses to all of these points have, of course, been made by various authorities, but none of them are totally convincing. With timely surgery, accident victims have survived far more serious injuries to the skull, heart and arteries and it is hard to accept that the reported French system of 'at the scene triage and initial stabilization' was the better option than a high-speed evacuation to the nearest hospital. In fact a US heart surgeon, Dr John Ochsner, has stated that Diana's pulmonary vein cannot have been as seriously damaged as claimed or she would have:

'...immediately died at the scene from loss of blood. The fact that she survived long enough to reach hospital suggests that the tear was minor.'

Again: if the ambulance was only travelling at 30mph, was it **really** necessary to stop just a short distance from the waiting surgeons at Pitie-Salpetriere to give an adrenalin injection?

What are we to make of all this? There are only a very limited number of possible explanations for the fact that Princess Diana's condition was allowed to deteriorate before she received proper medical care at a hospital **just three miles from the accident scene**:

- The French medical personnel involved all made critically poor judgments that delayed rapid access to an operating theatre and respirator.
- There was/is something fundamentally wrong with the French accident and emergency strategy of on-the-spot triage.

THE CONSPIRACY CONSPIRACY

- Very soon after the authorities were notified of Diana's involvement in a high-speed car crash, ***someone*** was able to influence decisions made and actions taken in order to turn a serious incident into a fatal one.

I submit to you once again the central principle of crime investigation:

MEANS, MOTIVE, OPPORTUNITY

If there is any substance to the belief that Diana, Princess of Wales, was allowed to die following a fortuitous road traffic accident, we have to concede that there are very few people

Plate 18: Alma Tunnel

or organizations with the power to ensure that the actions of the French emergency services made it certain.

The death of David Kelly

It has been established to most people's satisfaction that the invasion of Iraq in 2003 was at best unwarranted and poorly-considered and at worst based on the intentional misleading of the United Nations, Parliament and the British people by PM Tony Blair and his close advisors.

The motivation for the invasion was the threat of imminent use of so-called 'Weapons of Mass Destruction' (WMDs) by the Iraqi leader Saddam Hussein. British and American intelligence claimed to have discovered evidence of the stock-piling of poison gases and biological weapons and the manufacture of missiles and long-range artillery to deliver them. Iraq's deployment of mustard gas, sarin and tabun during its long war with neighbouring Iran and in attacks on its own Kurdish population were given as examples of its leadership's readiness to ignore international conventions on the use of chemical agents.

The Chilcot Report, published in July 2016, found that Saddam Hussein's forces had posed "no imminent threat" at the time, and that the invasion of Iraq in 2003 was based on "flawed" intelligence. It further declared that the cabinet's decision to invade was made in circumstances that were "far from satisfactory".

THE CONSPIRACY CONSPIRACY

A major embarrassment to Tony Blair was the leaking of a document to the BBC accusing the government of 'sexing up' its dossier on WMDs. The document claimed that the evidence for their existence was far from secure and that the risk posed by them had been greatly exaggerated. The source of this document was revealed to be Dr David Kelly, a government chemical weapons expert and former UN weapons inspector.

On July 18th, 2003 Dr Kelly's body was discovered in countryside near his home in Longworth, Oxfordshire, just two days after he had answered a summons to appear before a parliamentary Foreign Affairs Select Committee. The Hutton Inquiry set up by the government to examine the circumstances of Kelly's death reported that he had committed suicide, dying from a combination of blood loss from the slitting of his left wrist, an overdose of co-proxamol and coronary arterial atherosclerosis (!)

Not purely because of its convenient outcome for the Blair government, there are several reasons to believe that this verdict failed to consider or report all the available evidence and is seen by many as an attempt to cover up a more sinister cause of death. Some controversial aspects include:

- At the time of the publication of his report, Lord Hutton decreed that the post-mortem results, photographs of Kelly's body and the scene of his alleged suicide should remain classified for seventy years. (This was later reversed by the Conservative government in October 2010).

- In 2009 some of the conclusions of the Hutton Report were attacked by a group of British doctors, who stated that **transverse** slitting of the wrist would not have resulted in sufficient blood-loss to cause death.
- The two paramedics Dave Bartlett and Vanessa Hunt, who examined Kelly's body at Harrowdown Hill, have stated that the amount of blood they found at the scene amounted to just a few drops on surrounding vegetation and '**a spot the size of a coin**' on the scientist's trousers. From their own experience they declared that they would have expected to have seen: '**Several pints of blood at the scene of** [this type] **of suicide**'.
- A Freedom of Information request in October 2007, disclosed that the knife with which Kelly allegedly killed himself had no fingerprints on it when found. This was also the case with the blister back of co-proxamol, from which Kelly had supposedly removed 29 tablets, and the mobile phone in his pocket.
- In 2010 ten coroners, pathologists and intensive care surgeons cast doubt on the causes of death given in the Hutton Report and called for another, more impartial enquiry. Jennifer Dyson, a retired pathologist, stated her opinion that Kelly's death was more likely to have been the result of a heart attack than suicide.

THE CONSPIRACY CONSPIRACY

- In 2017, Kelly's body was exhumed and reportedly cremated, apparently at the request of his family, who were concerned that 'conspiracists' might themselves remove the body for autopsy. Of course, this action also prevented a more impartial investigation into the causes of the scientist's death.
- Lord Hutton was asked to carry out the enquiry into Kelly's death just three hours after his body was found: at that time neither the identity of the victim nor cause of death had been established.
- The request was made by Lord Falconer, a personal friend and former flatmate of Tony Blair, who is known to have spoken twice to Blair between 12.10 and 12.30, while the Premier was on a plane travelling from Washington to Tokyo. The timing coincides with Falconer's call to Hutton, inviting him to carry out the enquiry.
- Once Hutton had agreed, Falconer (then Lord Chancellor) used his powers to substitute the more usual coroner's inquest with a non-statutory public inquiry.
- Falconer was one of Tony Blair's closest advisors and was involved in over-ruling warnings that the invasion of Iraq could be an illegal act.

Whether Dr Kelly committed suicide (which seems very unlikely), died of a heart attack or was murdered to prevent him making further allegations (as suggested by conflicting forensic testimony and lack of fingerprints on important items of evidence) his death remains both contentious and extremely convenient for the authors of a war of dubious legality that resulted in the destabilisation of the entire Middle East.

Chemtrails

Any aircraft burning hydrocarbon fuels produces exhaust gases containing carbon dioxide and water: as an example, here's the equation for the burning of propane

$C_3H_8 + 5O_2 = 3CO_2 + 4H_2O$

propane + oxygen = carbon dioxide + water

Kerosene, the fuel used by jet aircraft, is a complex mixture of hydrocarbons with much larger molecules than propane but the products of combustion are identical.

$2C_{12}H_{26} + 37O_2 = 24CO_2 + 26H_2O$

A cruising multi-engined airliner produces around seven tonnes of water per hour, in the form of water vapour. Depending on the height at which the aircraft is flying and the external temperature, this will frequently condense to form droplets that may freeze into ice crystals. Water vapour already present in the upper atmosphere will be cooled by the contrail and add to its volume, producing the familiar 'contrail'. (It has been calculated that only one ten-thousandth of the water in a contrail comes from an aircraft's jet exhaust).

Both the US and UK governments have admitted that

THE CONSPIRACY CONSPIRACY

they carried out clandestine aerial spraying of 'harmless' agents over populated areas during the cold war, sometimes by injecting chemicals into jet exhausts.

Furthermore, it was acknowledged that aircraft were used in similar experiments on climate modification. This disclosure has been seized upon (perhaps not surprisingly!) by 'conspiracists' as evidence that the procedure continues today, the difference being that there is now something a lot more sinister about what is being sprayed and why.

The 'Chemtrail Conspiracy' suggests that US and UK military aircraft (and possibly even civil airliners) are routinely dosing the population with live microbial agents, toxic chemicals and possibly even psychoactive drugs. As proof of this, believers point to the sudden appearance of new viruses on an almost annual basis, the proliferation of several types of cancer and an increase in psychosis and other mental illnesses.

All of these are easily refuted: the pressures of modern life (and improved diagnosis of mental illness), the wider availability of intercontinental air travel and increased life expectation in the west probably contribute to all the above.

However, some of the 'chemtrail evidence' that has been collected is certainly worth a closer look.

I am fortunate enough to live in one of the 'driest' areas of the UK, averaging less than forty days rain annually. Since I maintain a daily wildlife blog and am a keen natural history photographer, I generally walk around 35 miles every week, setting off shortly after dawn most days. Soon after I began this routine ten years ago, I noticed an interesting daily phenomenon that has continued to the present day.

If, in the spring and summer, the early morning is completely blue and cloudless, US military aircraft often begin to appear: soon the sky is criss-crossed with contrails. These rapidly spread and join up, forming a thick haze. Within an hour there is frequently an eight okta layer of cirro-stratus clouds which may thicken and descend to cover the whole sky.

This happens so frequently that these USAF overflights **must** be affecting the regional climate. This of course, begs

Plate 19: Cloud cover sequence

the question: is this process intentional or accidental?

Given the presence of the twin USAF bases at Mildenhall and Lakenheath, and Norwich's busy civil airport, the volume of air traffic is, perhaps, not unexpected. It would seem likely that the dense east-bound military traffic around dawn could be transport aircraft carrying materiel onwards to USAF bases in Europe: certainly the majority seem to be C130s and C17s on their way to Ramstein, with KC135 and KC10 tanker aircraft from Mildenhall also frequent visitors.

None of which, of course, proves that these aircraft don't have a hidden agenda in addition to their routine missions!

Personally, I believe that the huge volume of jet transport around the globe has an unintended major impact on the weather: not because of the vast carbon dioxide emissions for which they are responsible, but rather as a result of the high altitude clouds of water vapour and ice crystals they produce. The grounding of all US civil aircraft for three days following the 911 attacks has been stated by some reputable researchers to have resulted in a two degree atmospheric temperature drop.

Other possibly linked phenomena are two rare cloud types, both of which occur at very high altitude and are thought by many to be the products of ice crystal and soot pollution from aircraft.

Displays of noctilucent and nacreous clouds are extremely beautiful and unusual events, only observed a few times a year. Since they became more common during the period when the US Space Shuttle fleet were still being launched regularly, it had been suggested that aluminium particles from the SRB (solid rocket booster) exhaust plumes might have

Plate 20: Noctilucent and nacreous cloud

been responsible. However, the closure of the program in July 2011 has not resulted in a reduction of either phenomenon, so their cause must lie elsewhere: possibly aviation.

The Fourth Reich
Did Hitler – or his dreams – survive World War 2?

Official accounts of the end of the Second World War state that Nazi leader Adolf Hitler (along with his new bride Eva Braun, security chief Joseph Goebbels and his wife and six children) died in a bunker beneath the embattled streets of Berlin.

For many years I've wondered whether an egocentric megalomaniac like Hitler would allow his life to come to such an ignominious end: surely he would have planned alternatives to suicide or capture by the Soviet Army well before the fall of Berlin?

The generally accepted evidence for Hitler's death is a fragment of skull and a piece of jawbone recovered by Russian forces near the Fuhrerbunker in 1945: however, DNA testing carried out in the United States in 2009 revealed that the skull fragment was that of a much younger **female**, while the only link between Hitler and the piece of jawbone is the verbal evidence of Hitler's dentist! There is compelling testimony that the partly-burned corpse found by the Russians and claimed to be that of the Nazi leader was in fact one of the numerous body doubles Hitler is known to have used.

Three key figures in any contingency plans for the escape

THE CONSPIRACY CONSPIRACY

Plate 21: Bormann, Skorzeny and Gehlen

of Hitler and other senior Nazis after the collapse of the Third Reich would have been S-Obersturmbannführer Otto Skorzeny, once described as 'the most dangerous man in Europe', General Reinhard Gehlen, commander of Foreign Armies East military-intelligence unit and Martin Bormann, Head of the Nazi Part Chancellery.

Martin Bormann

The death of Martin Bormann, most probably by suicide, was not 'confirmed' until 1998, when DNA testing was carried out on a skeleton discovered in 1972. Until then, intelligence agencies around the world had assumed that Bormann (together with other leading Nazis) had managed to break out of Berlin and escape, most probably to South America. His position of trust and influence within Hitler's closest circle meant that Bormann would certainly have been involved in any plans for Hitler's escape and it has been suggested that he was involved with Reichsfuhrer Heinrich Himmler in establishing **Odessa** (Organization Der Ehemaligen SS-Angehörigen). The formation of a group or groups for expediting the escape of senior Nazis and former SS members is absolutely certain: notorious war criminals that successfully fled Germany with the help of such an organisation include Adolf Eichmann and Josef Mengele. However, the existence of Odessa itself (despite many references to it in films, popular fiction and biographies) has been denied by US intelligence agencies.

It is strongly suspected that as early as 1944 Bormann had established mechanisms for evacuating himself, Hitler and others through Austria to Italy, via Spain, or by U-Boat. A number of very credible witnesses claim to have encountered Bormann in South America: in 1966 legendary Nazi hunter Simon Wiesenthal stated that he was certain Bormann was living in the Argentine-Chile border region under the name Ricardo Bauer.

But what about the eye-witness accounts of Bormann's death near the Lehrter Station, Berlin and the mDNA tests on the skeleton found in 1972? Well, the eye-witnesses were both Nazis with, perhaps, vested interests in supporting the idea that Bormann was dead, while the conveniently-discovered skeleton could have been secretly returned to Germany after Bormann's death in South America. It has been claimed that dental work identified as being carried out on Bormann during the war shows evidence of modern techniques performed **post mortem** and that distinctive red soil found on the skull can only be found in Paraguay. It is, perhaps, significant that after testing, 'Bormann's' remains were cremated and disposed of at sea (somewhat reminiscently of the hasty disposal of Osama Bin Laden's body!).

Otto Skorzeny

Born in Austria, Skorzeny (who was an officer in Hitler's bodyguard, the Leibstandarte) rose through the ranks of the SS and served on the Eastern Front. In 1942, following a serious head wound, he returned to Germany, where he developed his theories on the training and deployment of commando units, ultimately being placed in charge of five battalions of combat troops. His daring exploits included the mountain-top rescue of Italian dictator Benito Mussolini by glider commandos, the capture of the son of Hungarian Regent Miklos Horthy and leading 'Operation Greif' units dressed in US uniforms and driving captured American vehicles during the 'Battle of the Bulge' in December 1944. Subsequently, as part of the '**Spinne**' organisation set up by Skorzeny and Reinhard Gehlen, similar false-flag units transported at least 600 Nazi escapees through allied lines to Austria and onwards after fighting ceased.

Despite being implicated in numerous war crimes (including the possible shooting of captured US soldiers during the Battle of the Bulge) and being tried at the Dachau Trials of

1947, Skorzeny was never convicted on any major charges: he avoided punishment or 'de-nazification' by escaping from the Darmstadt internment camp, with the assistance, he claimed, of US military intelligence. It is considered possible that the **Spinne** network organised Hitler's escape to the Canary Islands, thence by U-Boat to Argentina.

Reinhard Gehlen

As mentioned in an earlier chapter, the American intelligence community showed no compunction against the recruitment of unreconstructed Nazis after World War Two: among these was Reinhard Gehlen, head of the Foreign Armies East (FHO) military-intelligence unit.

Rising to the rank of Major-General, Gehlen survived a 1944 dismissal by Hitler, who was angered by his 'defeatist' (but completely accurate) assessment of the fighting on the Eastern Front. Like Skorzeny, Gehlen was never tried as a high-ranking Nazi, but instead was recruited by US intelligence to undertake espionage against the Soviet Union. The Gehlen Organisation (AKA 'The Org') was subsumed by the CIA as part of its anti-soviet intelligence network, before being handed across to West Germany in 1956. Until 1968, Gehlen was chief of the Federal Intelligence Service, (the Bundesnachrichtendienst).

With Otto Skorzeny, Gehlen played a major part in the escape of many former Nazis and their assimilation into sympathetic communities around the world. The fact that Gehlen was not executed following his dismissal suggests that an agreement might have been reached, whereby Hitler's possible future use of Gehlen's network of contacts and clandestine transport was exchanged for his survival from the charge of defeatism.

The post-war careers of two of these high-ranking Nazis and the probable survival of the third, together with their involvement in setting up organizations to assist numerous war criminals to flee justice, makes it seem likely that they would have involved in any plan for Hitler's post-war escape.

If Hitler **was** passed along the **Spinne** 'spider web', what was his eventual destination and what happened after he arrived?

Contrary to what orthodoxy would have us believe, there is actually quite an amount of suggestive evidence that Hitler was transported to Argentina in a submarine, that he was secretly welcomed by President Juan Peron and lived there among a community of escaped Nazis for ten or more years. When the situation in Argentina altered, it is claimed that Hitler and others moved onward to Uruguay, living until 1971 under the protection of President Alfred Stroessner.

If both Hitler and Bormann survived the defeat of Germany and, together with vast amounts of unaccounted Nazi money, established a clandestine Nazi community in South America, what were its aims?

It is a possible scenario that, realizing the futility of attempting the *military* subjugation of Europe, the Nazi leadership in exile changed their strategy into one of political,

THE CONSPIRACY CONSPIRACY

industrial and economic conquest. It is observably the case that the reunification of Germany and the global influence of its current Chancellor, Angela Merkel (often described as the most powerful woman in the world) has left the country as the *de facto* leader of a modern Europe that currently includes large parts of the former Soviet Union. It was the allied rebuilding of West German industry, the protection of the country by the forces of NATO (both at huge expense) and the success of its Gehlen-based intelligence service that, it could be argued, have allowed this 'Fourth Reich' to achieve most of Hitler's aims.

Chapter 9: In conclusion...

IF you've managed to read this far, you may have arrived at your own opinions about this book. You may feel it is:

- A good read: 'chewing gum for the brain and eyes', not to be taken too seriously. A 'nice little earner' for the author!
- The ramblings of a grumpy old cynic, based upon nothing but outmoded and irrational prejudices.
- Cleverly-assembled half-truths intended to persuade and mislead its readership for sinister hidden motives.
- A partly true assessment of the way that the media occasionally manipulates historical and current affairs for political and propaganda advantage.
- All true: the book reflects what you have long suspected yourself.

In fact, I know exactly why I laboriously tapped out the book (with two fingers and two thumbs!) at '**What time are you coming to bed**?' o'clock. Like almost everything I have written (seven books, twenty-plus short stories and

THE CONSPIRACY CONSPIRACY

hundreds of magazine articles) I have earned hardly any financial reward. But that was never my motivation: hardly anyone apart from Dan Brown and Lee Child makes any money from book sales these days!

In the film **'JFK'**, the Kevin Costner character, District Attorney Jim Garrison, includes the following in his summing up at the end of the trial scene:

"I'm 45, so there's no hope for me, but I'm already training my eight-year-old son to keep himself physically fit so that on one glorious September morn in 2038 he can walk into the National Archives in Washington and find out what the CIA knew about Lee Harvey Oswald. If there's a further extension of the top-secret classification, this may become a generational affair, with questions passed down from father to son in the manner of the ancient runic bards"

That's why I write: to try and ensure that data from all sides of the argument of as many controversial events as possible is available for future debate.

Since I first took the opportunity to talk with the eighteen astronauts who allegedly took part in the six lunar landings, ten have died (at the time of writing). The youngest of the 'Moonwalkers', Gen. Charles Duke, was born in 1935, so it doesn't take much reflection to realise that soon there won't be anyone left to give a first-hand account of 'Mankind's greatest adventure' – one way or another!

As a legal deposit library, the British Library receives copies of all books produced in the United Kingdom and Ireland, including this one and all my previous publications: I believe copies of these have also been deposited in some quite surprising collections, both here and abroad.

So while I will never achieve immortality, at least some of my ideas will! If any of the material I have presented above has caused you to think, ask questions and maybe even carry out your own research, I will have achieved my goal . . .

THE CONSPIRACY CONSPIRACY

APPENDIX 1:

POPULAR evidence for the reality of the Moon landings – refuted!

I could talk for hours about the inconsistencies and scientific inaccuracies that pervade the official record of the six alleged Moon landings. When I give lectures on the subject, the most frequent pieces of 'supportive evidence' I'm presented with are:

- *Scientists around the world still measure the distance to the Moon by reflecting laser beams from a mirror left on the surface by the Apollo 11 Moonwalkers.*

    Sounds conclusive! However, because the Moon has a high albedo people have been bouncing lasers off the lunar surface since 1957. Also, both the Russians and Americans have soft-landed unmanned probes from as far back as 1966: any of these could have laser reflectors mounted on them.

- *The Apollo astronauts brought back three minerals that are unknown on Earth: Armalcolite, Tranquillityite and Pyroxferroite.*

    This was alleged to be the case at the time: these

THE CONSPIRACY CONSPIRACY

have now all been found on Earth. (In fact I sell displays containing all three!)

- *The Apollo Moon rocks have been analysed in independent laboratories and been found to be different to anything found on Earth.*

  Even if this were true (and it isn't!) the vast majority of the Apollo samples – well over 300kg – have never been examined by independent researchers, being 'archived for posterity' at the Lunar Sample Laboratory Facility at the Johnson Space Center, Houston, Texas. The few samples made available to other researchers are carefully monitored during their time away from Houston. Perhaps significantly, since the Apollo Program ended in 1972 well over 100 **meteorites** have been identified as being lunar in origin: many of these are also stored at the LSLF! At the time of writing their total mass is 212kg: how could a researcher be sure of the origin of a rock claimed to have been collected by the Apollo astronauts?

- *The Apollo astronauts were protected from harmful radiation by their spacecraft's heavy shielding: in any case the passage through the Van Allen Belts took only two hours.*

  Oh really? The Apollo Command Module in which the astronauts spent over six days in cislunar space had two 'skins': an inner layer of aluminium sheet

THE CONSPIRACY CONSPIRACY

and honeycomb and a similar outer layer made from stainless steel, The **total** thickness varied from an extreme of six inches at the base to a minimum of **three quarters of an inch** elsewhere. Bearing in mind that radiation would pass straight through the honeycomb elements that made up most of the thickness: would this be your choice for a six-day exposure to solar and cosmic radiation and high energy particles?

Then there's the situation with Apollo 13! As we all know from the eponymous film about the mission, the three astronauts spent most of the 2 day 15 hour return journey from their 'slingshot' around the Moon in the Lunar Module (to conserve battery power!) In his book 'A Man On The Moon' author Andrew Chaikin wrote:

"In the ascent stage, the walls of the crew cabin were thinned down until they were nothing more than a taut aluminum balloon, in some places only **five-thousandths of an inch thick.** Once, a workman accidentally dropped a screwdriver inside the cabin and it went through the floor."

It should also be recalled that the Apollo 17 astronauts spent close to 75 hours on the Moon: an airless world offering no protection from constant high energy particles and radiation. This lack of shielding seems a little risky, given that just four

THE CONSPIRACY CONSPIRACY

months before the landing, a huge Coronal Mass Ejection swept the lunar surface that would have killed all three astronauts instantly.

- *'The brightness of the lunar surface and of the Sun and Earth made it impossible [for the Moonwalkers] to see stars: this was also true in cislunar space.'* (Neil Armstrong)

Oh really? Perhaps the Apollo 11 commander should have mentioned this to Apollo 14 LM Pilot Dr Edgar Mitchell, who frequently commented on how bright the stars were when seen from the Moon's surface. And as for cislunar space: the success of the entire program depended upon accurate star-sightings to make mid-course corrections! The Apollo 13 film includes a dramatic section where clouds of ice and debris prevent Jim Lovell from locating the stars he needs to do so.

THE CONSPIRACY CONSPIRACY

APPENDIX 2:

'EXPLANATIONS' of the Rendlesham Forest UFO – dismissed!

- *Over three days the numerous eyewitnesses were deceived by the flashing beam of the Orford Lighthouse.*

    Many of those who claim to have experienced the events of December 1980 saw a strange craft at close range: one even describes touching it. Many of the witnesses had been based in the area for several years and were entirely familiar with the lighthouse and the nearby Shipwash Lightship.

- *The initial witnesses actually saw a Soviet satellite burning up as it re-entered the atmosphere.*

    Nobody has been able to provide a name for this satellite, nor evidence that such an event occurred.

- *The so-called UFO was an exploding fireball: these are frequently reported as extraterrestrial craft.*

    No they are not! Even in these days of somewhat patchy science provision in schools, most people

THE CONSPIRACY CONSPIRACY

know what meteors, bolides and fireballs look like. Although a bright fireball **was** recorded over southern England that winter, there are no accounts of it being seen as far north as Suffolk: in any case, the date of the fireball doesn't coincide with those of the RFI.

- *The whole event was based around the misinterpretation of a 'secret training exercise' involving Apollo 'boilerplate capsule.' BP-1206, which was accidentally dropped into the woods from a helicopter operated by the US 67th ARRS (Air Rescue and Recovery Squadron).*

Nice try! Unfortunately BP-1206 had been sent back to the United States three years earlier. Also: meteorological records reveal that the nights in question were too foggy for flight operations to take place.

- *Kevin Conde, a former military police officer at the base admits the whole thing was a hoax he perpetrated on a 'gullible' member of the gate security team, using a 1979 Plymouth Volare decked out with strobing coloured lights.*

Conde's story only emerged over twenty years after the Rendlesham Forest UFO incident. Furthermore, he talks of driving his police car along the **taxiway** at Woodbridge: the first night witnesses at the

THE CONSPIRACY CONSPIRACY

base's East Gate initially observed lights moving through the **forest.**

- *A well-known sceptic has claimed that the manufacturers of the radiation detector used in the forest on the second night of events has stated that the radiation levels recorded were 'of little or no significance'.*

The levels claimed by Lt Col Halt, the Deputy Base Commander who led the investigating team into the forest, peaked at .1mR/h (milliroentgens per hour) which is around eight times the normal background count. This **is** insignificant if we are discussing evidence of a major radiation leak, but we are not! No-one **ever** claimed that the Rendlesham Forest UFO was powered by some form of nuclear reactor. Stating that this level is of no significance is like saying that traces of DNA evidence at a murder scene are of no importance!

THE CONSPIRACY CONSPIRACY

Appendix 3:

INTRODUCED **or invasive species that threaten native flora and fauna.**

Most people would be surprised to discover just how many of our 'wild' plants and animals are actually alien species that have been released intentionally, have escaped from private collections or which have made it to the UK under their own steam! The few listed below have not been subjected to a successful programme of eradication like that of the Ruddy Duck, despite the threat they pose to our indigenous wildlife and ecosystems. (The Ruddy Duck only poses a claimed threat to the wildlife of Spain!).

- The Grey Squirrel: introduced into parks, estates and large gardens in the 1870s, this North American species has been flagged as the major factor in the rapidly diminishing population of the Red Squirrel.
- The Mink is an aggressive North American mustelid that has been linked with a rapid decline in the number of Water Voles in the UK since its release or escape in the early twentieth century.

THE CONSPIRACY CONSPIRACY

- The Chinese Water Deer and Muntjac are small species of deer that were introduced by the Duke of Bedford onto his Woburn Estate: some escaped into the wild after the Second World War and both species are increasing in numbers throughout the eastern counties. It is not yet clear what the long-term impact of the two species will be, but both eat farm crops and both are implicated in 'stressing out' ground-nesting birds such as Stone Curlews and Bitterns.
- The Rhododendron is a familiar flowering shrub of parks and gardens: it was a British native before the last Ice Age, but all plants in the UK are introduced species. One of these, *Rhododendron ponticum*, occurs in southern and eastern Europe and, since its cultivation here, has become a serious problem in many parts of the UK. It spreads rapidly, is very difficult to eradicate and can eliminate native shrubs and herbs.
- The Red-legged Partridge is a small non-native game bird that is released in vast numbers by gamekeepers every year. It is native to the Mediterranean region and was introduced in the eighteenth century. Since it can produce two parallel broods every year, it has spread widely over the drier areas of the UK, where it has been implicated in the decline of the native Grey Partridge.

THE CONSPIRACY CONSPIRACY

- The Zander, Carp and Wels Catfish are all introductions that have had major impacts on the populations of some native fish. Originally found only in a few lakes, illegal transfers and escapes to river systems have allowed these (and other alien species) to spread widely and affect native fish stocks with which they compete.
- The Canada Goose is a species that was originally introduced into park and estate lakes from North America. Together with the Greylag and Egyptian Goose it has rapidly increased its range and population. Unlike other species of ornamental wildfowl species such as the Mandarin Duck and Muscovy, these now constitute a significant problem in some areas: all three hybridise with native geese species.

THE CONSPIRACY CONSPIRACY

Acknowledgments and Thanks

As always: above all, thanks to my beautiful wife and best friend **Linda**. She has always been the first to encourage me to put my ideas into print, and the first to point out the occasional errors in my logic!

My older brother **Dr Rob Bryant** remains my long-suffering sounding board. He has always been the first person I have asked to read my initial drafts: inevitably he and his many contacts in professional and academic Science have had their work cut out with the present volume!

Many, many thanks to **Ray Kohn**, who I first met at Cambridge nearly fifty years ago: despite family pressures and being a very busy man, he kindly agreed to read the book and write a foreword. Ray is a genuine renaissance man: violinist, author, philosopher, educational theorist and composer. Here's his website: **http://raykohn.com/**

Thanks to **Bob Tibbitts**, my 'go-to' typesetter and editor: he encourages me in my efforts and gently explains what is and what is not possible!

Lastly: thanks to our dear friends **Sue** and **Peter Rowe** who (despite personal and professional reservations about many of my ideas) have been ever-ready to listen to them and give constructive criticism where necessary (usually over a glass of wine). Thanks also to birding chums **Brian Tubby** and **Norman Tottle** for their interest in my writing and for the many animated discussions we have enjoyed together.

Bibliography

Ray Kohn: *'Enforced Leisure: enforced education'*, Fabian Society, 1982

Col. Philip J. Corso: *'The Day after Roswell'*, Pocket Books, 1997

John Hanson & Charles Irwin Halt: *'The Halt Perspective'*, Haunted Skies Publishing, 2016

Simon Dunstan & Gerrard Williams: *'The Grey Wolf'*, Sterling, 2012

David Icke: *'The Biggest Secret'*, Bridge of Love Publications, 1998

Robert J Groden: *'The Killing of a President'*, Viking Studio Books, 1994

Henrik Svensmark & Nigel Calder: *'The Chilling Stars'*, Cambridge Icon Books, 2007

David Bellamy: *'Conflicts in the Countryside: The New Battle for Britain'*, 2005, Shaw & Sons

Ian Wishart: *'Totalitaria: What If The Enemy Is The State?'*, 2013, Howling At The Moon Publishing Ltd

THE CONSPIRACY CONSPIRACY

Glossary

Albedo
This is a measure of the degree to which a body or surface reflects solar radiation, from 0 (black) to 1 (white).

Anthropology
This is the scientific study of human societies, and their cultures and development, and of the evolution of human biological and physiological characteristics.

Boilerplate Capsule
Designed to simulate the weight and external characteristics of the Apollo Command Module, these full-sized replicas were used primarily to train units in recovery techniques, but also during design and fitting out operations.

Cislunar/cis-lunar space
This is the volume of space that would be enclosed by a sphere centred on the Earth with the Earth-Moon distance as its radius.

CM/Command Module
The CM is the crew compartment of any spacecraft constructed in several parts. In the case of the Gemini and Apollo spacecraft, the astronauts spent most of their time in the CM

THE CONSPIRACY CONSPIRACY

and returned to Earth inside it. Soviet / Russian spacecraft feature a similar re-entry capsule.

CME: Coronal Mass Ejection

An emission of billions of tons of particles from the Sun's corona, travelling at millions of kilometres per hour. These high energy emissions can disrupt radio and TV transmissions on Earth and even cause electrical power grids to shut down.

Type 2 Diabetes

This condition is characterised by raised blood sugar levels, generally caused either when the body fails to produce enough insulin, or develops a resistance to the hormone. It can be controlled by drugs, diet, exercise or a combination of all three.

Genotype

The genetic 'make up' of any cell or organism, encoded on the DNA that makes up the chromosomes found in virtually all living cells. The physical appearance and some of the behaviour of an organism are predicated by its genotype.

Lunar Module/LM/LEM

The curiously-shaped Lunar Module was designed to carry two astronauts (the Commander and Lunar Module Pilot) to the surface of the Moon, provide living accommodation for the duration of the visit and return the astronauts to lunar orbit, where they would rendezvous with the Command Module. Except in the case of Apollo 13, the Lunar Module was not used for long-duration spaceflight and offered little resistance to radiation or micro-meteorite impact.

THE CONSPIRACY CONSPIRACY

Megalodon
Carcharodon megalodon was a giant relative of the Great White Shark that is generally considered to have become extinct around 2.6 million years ago. However, credible sightings of surviving individuals are occasionally reported.

Meteoritics
This is the branch of Astronomy and Planetary Geology concerned with meteorites and other extraterrestrial material that reach the Earth from space.

Mustelid
One of a group of small, typically ferocious mammal that includes Weasels, Mink, Otters, Badgers, Polecats and Wolverines

Phenotype
The physical appearance of an organism, the result of the interaction between its DNA and the environment

Pulmonary Veins
Two pulmonary veins emerge from each lung, and carry oxygenated blood into the left atrium of the heart. Each lung has an inferior and superior vein so there are four pulmonary veins in total.

QCA
The Qualifications and Curriculum Authority is a non-departmental public body, sponsored by the Department for Education and Skills, which produces syllabi, examination papers and tests associated with the National Curriculum.

Regolith

This is the term used for a layer of crushed rock, dust and debris over a solid surface, typically found on the Moon, Mars, asteroids and other bodies that have been subject to major impact events.

Thermite Reaction

The chemical reaction between powdered aluminium and a metal oxide can be extremely exothermic (producing a lot of heat). A thermite reaction involving iron oxide is often used as a method of local welding, such as joining pieces of rail track.

DISCLAIMER

Although every precaution has been taken in the preparation of this book, the publisher and author assume no responsibility for errors or omissions. Neither is any liability assumed for damages resulting from the use of the information contained within. All images are either the copyright of the author or are in the public domain, in which case credit has been given.

 SPACEROCKS UK

DAVID BRYANT, BSc, Cert Ed is the only full-time meteorite dealer in England. His company 'Spacerocks UK' holds a complete inventory of all meteorite types, from 4.5 billion year old common chondrites, to iron meteorites, rare and beautiful pallasites and even pieces of the Moon, Mars and the Asteroid Vesta!

He is a member of the IMCA, (International Meteorite Collectors Association) and all his items are sold with an A4 factsheet and guarantee of authenticity. David has delivered lectures about meteorites at meetings of the British Astronomical Association, the Society for Popular Astronomy, for the BBC's 'Stargazing Live' events and astronomical societies all over the country.

David sells his meteorites at rock and mineral shows around the UK, from Cambridgeshire to Devon and at most of his public lectures.

All these items can be purchased by 'phone, 01603 715933

or from the SPACEROCKS UK website at:
http://www.spacerocksuk.com
email: info@spacerocksuk.com

His wife, Linda, makes a wide range of beautiful meteorite and impactite jewellery using solid silver chains and findings, which are available from her website:
http://www.space-jewellery.co.uk

OUR FORBIDDEN MOON By David Bryant *(Foreword by Nick Pope)*
136 pages, some in colour

David Bryant's book *Our Forbidden Moon* has taken fifteen years of meticulous planning and research to write. During encounters with over thirty astronauts and cosmonauts, including seven of the twelve alleged Moonwalkers, the author gradually became aware of a number of major inconsistencies in their recollections of the Apollo program. Furthermore, in occasional unguarded moments, several space travellers have revealed personal experiences of the UFO phenomenon and hinted at even more dramatic events. *Our Forbidden Moon* examines these revelations and considers whether there might be a link between UFOs, extraterrestrial races and mankind's forty-year failure to travel beyond low Earth orbit. The author uses his knowledge gained during forty years as a teacher, lecturer and respected authority on spaceflight and meteoritics to ask controversial questions and provide convincing solutions.

UNINVITED COMPANIONS By David Bryant *(Foreword by Lionel Fanthorpe)*
166 pages, some in colour

Uninvited Companions is an examination of the paranormal phenomena known as orbs: the strange spheres of light that frequently appear on video and still photographs or are even, at times, seen by the unaided eye. With a BSc in Biological Sciences and Astronomy and a lifetime as a teacher and lecturer, author David Bryant has reached some new and startling conclusions about these contentious objects! The book examines other, apparently unrelated paranormal happenings, and consider whether they might be linked in some way to the orb phenomenon.

DANGER FROM THE SKIES By David Bryant *(Foreword by Dr Rob Bryant)*
136 pages, some in colour

Danger from the Skies! Are catastrophic impacts upon the Earth's surface the major driving-force of Evolution? Cuvier vs Darwin: do we need to revise our understanding of the Origin of Species? Are asteroids really a significant threat to life on Earth? Or is their role in extinction over-stated? Is mankind's nemesis lurking unsuspected far beyond the orbits of Neptune and Pluto? When can we expect another major extinction event and what can we do to prevent it?

www.ingramcontent.com/pod-product-compliance
Lightning Source LLC
Chambersburg PA
CBHW081156020426
42333CB00020B/2523